DISCOVERING BRITAIN'S FIRST RAILWAYS

A GUIDE TO HORSE-DRAWN TRAMROADS AND WAGGONWAYS

MARK JONES

The History Press

First published 2012

The History Press
The Mill, Brimscombe Port,
Stroud, Gloucestershire, GL5 2QG
www.thehistorypress.co.uk

British Library Cataloguing in Publication Data.
A catalogue record for this book is available from the British Library.

ISBN 978 0 7524 6273 8

Typesetting and origination by The History Press
Printed in Great Britain

Contents

Acknowledgements

I would like to acknowledge all the help and support I have received in the preparation of this book. Such support has come in many forms. Let me first thank all those who have supplied photographs: Richard Lewis; Phillip Earnshaw; Leslie Oppitz; Chris McFarlane; Gordon Suggitt; Robin Willis from the Penrhyn Railway Society; Howard Harrison; Steve Gilligan; John Simmonds; and most of all the Railway & Canal Historical Society in their role as custodians of the Bertram Baxter Collection. In that regard, I wish to express my gratitude to the late John Wooldridge for allowing me to sift through and select from Mr Baxter's photographs. I would also like to thank Marc Alexander and the late Paul Abrahams for allowing use of the base map seen on page 8.

So many people have freely given their time to offer more general advice and information. I would especially like to thank Jeff Vinter; Mike Hodgson; Brian Slater; Bernard Parkinson; Debbie Dewhurst; Gerald Leach; Roger Taylor; Graham Bird; and particularly the late Ralph Rawlinson.

Finally and most importantly I would like to thank my son Connor for accompanying me on various trips to far-flung parts of the country; and for putting up with my not infrequent absences from my family responsibilities.

Introduction

To discover 'Britain's first railways' is to open the door into a secret and little-known world. Let us start with what is familiar – the current rail network, largely unchanged in size over the last thirty to forty years but with locomotives now almost entirely superseded by the ubiquitous 'units' that provide nearly all our passenger services these days. A growing number of us are also familiar with the ever-increasing network of 'railway paths', converted lines given a second life as paths and trails which can be walked and cycled, many of which developed following the wholesale closure of unprofitable railways – not by any means all minor branch lines – ordered by Dr Beeching in the 1960s (though some closures took place in the 1950s and early 1960s and are incorrectly blamed on Beeching, whose first report appeared in 1962). A few of these lines were 'early' and will be discussed further in later chapters.

So what do we mean by 'Britain's first railways'? Our working definition will be those that pre-date the use of steam locomotives – meaning, in simple terms, those that were at least for a short time powered by horse. All the lines we consider in the final chapter of the book were at one time horse drawn, though some were converted to steam haulage and others, for varying reasons, were opened rather later, but 'first railways' will serve us perfectly well. These early railways are the subject of surprisingly little literature, particularly compared to the weight of volumes on canals and locomotive-hauled railways, although many books on individual lines exist, the result of much painstaking research, which have provided valuable sources of information for this book. The one exception, and one that I will make no apologies for referring to frequently in the forthcoming pages, is *Stone Blocks and Iron Rails* by Bertram Baxter. Although nearly fifty years old, long since out of print and not easy to find in the second-hand book market, it remains a standard and valuable text, particularly for those who would like more detail on the historical aspects and principals of operation of our routes that this book can provide.

In researching this book and having access to Mr Baxter's photographs, maps, documents and private correspondence, the author became very aware of how the process of collecting, processing and making use of information has changed over the years. Baxter studied old tramroads in great detail from the late 1920s until his somewhat premature death in the early 1960s. Whilst in those days there was obviously more left to see on the ground, recorded in several thousand carefully labelled photographs (a selection of which I am fortunate to be able to reproduce in this volume), the collecting of historical and operational details was far more laborious than it might be today. Baxter would contact librarians and archivists by letter, who would then work their way for him through old records, newspapers and any other written sources available. Few formal records would survive as sources of information as the original companies were either taken over by the railways, closed down or, in some places, just faded away without ever having gone through a formal winding-up process. Through the exchange of letters, Mr Baxter became friends with many of his 'contributors', and the letters at times also give glimpses of a gradual development of informality and of his lifestyle in general.

I have not attempted to replicate the remarkable gazetteer that Baxter compiled, including many tiny lines of less than half a mile in length. Comprehensive though it was, there are a number of possible omissions: Baxter did not mention the Caughly Railway near Ironbridge in Shropshire, nor did he include any tramways in Yorkshire associated with the Leeds & Liverpool Canal, other than one running down to the canal at Skipton.

So, what is this book's purpose? Firstly we will look at the very early days of transport, how rails developed, why they are useful and why they met the requirements better than any alternatives. We will look at the developing need for transport as the Industrial Revolution gained strength and the large amounts of materials needed to be brought in and out of mills, factories and indeed whole towns. We will look at how these lines were constructed and operated, the materials that were used and how in many places they linked with and effectively extended the nation's system of canals. Alongside our main narrative we will see how the development of locomotives and, perhaps more importantly, improvements in track construction allowed these heavy 'iron horses' to safely run on them.

The second part of this volume will examine how to look for and discover old tramroads, where they were built and what remains of them to explore today. Much infrastructure, including viaducts and tunnels as well as trackbed and earthworks, remains to be discovered (in a personal sense) by those who know where to look for it. A number can now be walked for a part (sometimes a large part) of their length; such lines are described in more detail in the second half of the book.

While becoming expert in the rise and decline of horse-drawn tramroads in Britain you will find yourself sharing in tales of national, not just local, significance. Join me now in a journey of exploration and discovery. So without more ado, lets get 'out there' and start discovering some early railways.

Mark Jones, 2012

Tramway and Waggonway Locations

1 Cornish Mineral Tramways: Portreath to Devoran
2 Treffry's Railway: Luxulyan to Ponts Mill
3 Plymouth & Dartmoor Railway
4 Haytor Granite Railway
5 Rattlebrook Peat Railway
6 Portland Railways
7 Purbeck Tramways
8 Somerset Coal Canal Tramway
9 Dramway: Coalpit Heath to Keynsham
10 Saundersfoot Railway
11 Swansea & Mumbles Railway
12 Carmarthenshire Railway
13 Hirwaun to Abernant and Penderyn Tramways
14 Brinore Tramroad: Talybont-on-Usk
15 Penydarren Tramway
16 Hill's Tramroad, Blaenavon
17 Brynmawr and Llangattock Tramways
18 Forest of Dean Railways
19 Brill Tramway
20 Peak Forest Tramway
21 Cromford & High Peak Railway
22 Caldon Low Tramways
23 Congleton Railway and Mow Cop Tramway
24 Nantlle Railway
25 Talyllyn Railway
26 Penrhyn Railway
27 Glyn Valley Tramway: Chirk
28 Storeton Tramway: Wirral
29 Walton Summit Plateway: Preston
30 Lord Carlisle's Railway: Lambley to Brampton
31 Edinburgh & Dalkeith Railway
32 Tranent to Cockenzie Waggonway
33 Silkstone Railway
34 Heck Bridge & Wentbridge Railway
35 Aberford Railway
36 Whitby & Pickering Railway
37 Waskerley Way
38 Tanfield Railway
39 Wylam Waggonway
40 Holy Island Waggonway

1

How Wheeled Transport Originated

Our look at early railways has to have a starting point, so let us start at the very beginning. To make the carriage of materials easier we need two things: a smooth, but not too smooth, surface for our 'carriage' to move on top of and something that can move fairly freely along our surface, a wheel or possibly a sledge. The former requirement we will come back to in a while.

So how did the 'wheel' come about? Tradition maintains that it was invented in Mesopotamia, but modern evidence suggests that a number of different civilisations developed it independently. Firstly, it was noticed that a heavy object could be moved more easily if something roughly round in cross section, for example a fallen tree log, was placed under it and the object rolled along over it. Alternatively a number of smaller logs or sticks could be placed under an object which would enable it to slide in the manner of a sledge.

The next development was to combine the two techniques. A number of logs, or rollers were placed in a row, and the object to be moved was dragged from one roller to the next. With time the 'sledges' started to wear grooves into the rollers and people noticed that the grooved rollers actually worked better, carrying the object further and requiring less effort. This was simple physics, if the unworn parts of the roller had a larger circumference than the grooves then dragging the sledge in the grooves required less energy to create a turning motion, but created a greater distance covered when the larger part of the log roller turned. The log roller had effectively become a wheel, and from there the next development was to cut away much of the wood between the two inner grooves to create what we can call an axle. Wooden pegs were used to fix the sledge, so that when it rested on the rollers it did not move, but allowed the axle to turn in between the pegs, so that the axles and the wheels now created all the movement. These were the first carts.

Improvements to the carts were gradually made. The pegs were replaced with holes carved into the cart frame so that the axle could be placed through the hole. This made it necessary for the larger wheels and thinner axle to be separate pieces. The wheels were attached to both sides of the axle. Next, the fixed axle was invented, where the axle does not turn but is solidly connected to the cart frame. Only the wheels did the revolving by being fitted onto the axle in a way that allowed them to rotate; these fixed axles made for stable carts that could turn corners better.

Let us now return to the subject of the 'road' surface. Although some old trackways are of Iron Age origin, our oldest surviving examples are those created by the Romans. In places such as Pompeii you can still see rows of streets where the cobbled surface of the road is heavily rutted from the waggon wheels. It is reasonable to assume that most carts would have had wheels the same distance apart, otherwise this rutting would not have occurred. Also if someone had a non-standard waggon, progress would have become much more difficult as one side would be in the rut and the other side not. There would therefore have been one standard 'gauge'. Having visited Pompeii in 2009, a year or so before this book was conceived, the author now very much wishes he had taken a tape measure with him to measure precisely what that gauge was, though it did look to be around 4–5ft in width, quite similar to what eventually became the 'standard gauge' on our railways. The cobbled, rutted and heavily cambered road surfaces were, and indeed still are, very uncomfortable to walk along, so horses and carts might well have been the choice of transport for quite short distances.

The issue of how far ancient Greeks and Romans managed to develop and harness steam power has long been a subject of debate amongst classical scholars. They were certainly aware that the process of producing steam was accompanied by some considerable force. The first known reference relates to 'Hero' of Alexandria, who in the first century AD produced a device called an 'Aeolipile' which was effectively a sealed cauldron, heated from below to build up a pressure of steam. The steam was then conveyed to a hollow ball spinning on a horizontal axis. Fixed to this ball were two L-shaped pipes opening in opposite directions which caused the ball to rotate rapidly, thus producing considerable energy.

Little evidence exists of other scientists of that time refining the 'engine' or in any way developing a use for such power. There was scant need, for Greek and Roman civilisations had an almost limitless supply of horses and slaves. Later the idea of steam propulsion became the subject of medieval science fiction – the thirteenth-century Somerset-born but Oxford-educated Roger Bacon wrote that, 'One day we shall endow chariots with incredible speed without the aid of any animal.' Erasmus Darwin, an eighteenth-century country doctor and incidentally grandfather of the great naturalist Charles Darwin, was also ahead of his time when predicting, 'Soon shall thy arm, unconquered steam! Afar drag the slow barge, or drive the rapid car'.

Returning to the 'surface', Britain's best surviving examples of Roman 'tracks' are on Blackstone Edge, east of Littleborough in Lancashire and forming part of what was once a route over the Pennines across Rishworth Moor towards Halifax or Elland in Yorkshire. The 'grooves' can clearly be seen on the ground, with cobbles between, though a disclaimer is necessary as no contemporary records of the road in use in Roman times have surfaced, and the first reference to it is not until the twelfth century. Roman roads were used by pedestrians, men on horseback and packhorses as well as carts (with two wheels) and waggons (four wheels). It seems likely that most if not all waggons would have been built with a common width between the wheels to allow for the use of the grooves.

After the Romans left Britain, the roads became regarded by locals as more of a threat – possibly bringing invaders or neighbouring warlike tribes – than a valuable trading asset. Consequently many roads were deliberated severed – perhaps the best known example of such 'vandalism' is the Bokerley Dyke which blocked a Roman road south of Salisbury in Wiltshire. As no maintenance or repairs were carried out, the roads gradually fell into disrepair. Heavy rain damaged culverts, bridges collapsed and side-drains filled with leaves and other debris so they could no longer fulfil their purpose. Houses were sometimes built where a good, dry surface remained, and in other places the stones were quarried and taken away for reuse elsewhere. Only certain upland tracks, where some natural drainage was available, managed to survive in anything like a usable condition.

It is not true to say that materials such as stone and coal were not quarried, mined and transported in medieval times, just that such material was, wherever possible, used close to where it was sourced. Good examples of these practices can be gleaned from historical records of activities in the Forest of Dean. Here rich deposits of iron ore were exploited by the Romans and later were supplied to ironworkers operating in Dean during the latter part of the eleventh century. Coal was being dug in several of the Forest's bailiwicks in the mid-1240s but its extraction was of secondary importance to ore mining until the seventeenth century. About 1250 the Crown received rents from some ore and coal mines taking ½d for every load of coal carried on the River Severn, or every load of ore taken out of the Forest.

It is clear that by the thirteenth century coal mining was a widely established 'industry', albeit generally in small-scale operations. It is reported that Queen Eleanor complained of the smell of smoke on a visit to Nottingham in 1257 and that a man was run over and killed by three horses hauling a 'coal cart' in nearby Breaston in 1290. By the fourteenth century coal was being taken into towns on two-wheeled carts, and there was also a growing need for somewhat larger vehicles to carry stone from its quarry to where it was needed to build houses, churches and the occasional bridge. Other roads started to be needed to serve growing towns of note such as Plymouth and Coventry, which had not been founded and developed by the Romans. Not all roads, though, were looked after; some were instead used as sources of clay. One road in Middlesex between Staines and Egham apparently had an 8ft deep 'pothole' into which at least one poor fellow fell and drowned. The fourteenth century did, however, see improvements in road maintenance in certain places due to the introduction of tolls.

Notwithstanding the above, by the time a demand for travel over longer distances had started to become a significant factor again, around the late seventeenth or early eighteenth century, the Roman roads still formed the backbone of the new network. Where it was not possible to use the original route a diversion had to be found, and it is worth noting that it is often possible for those interested in discovering the remains of Roman roads to find them here. The best method is to identify a known Roman road, find a point at which the modern road deviates from the original straight route and then look for the Roman remains by following the original alignment. However, some roads remained in an almost unbelievably poor condition; it was reported that during the English Civil War in the 1640s, Lord Leven complained that roads in Herefordshire were so difficult to traverse that his troops could manage no more than 8 miles in one day.

So we can see that, largely due to the poor road conditions until the 1700s, transportation in Britain relied either on the horse, on water, or indeed a human being's own feet. As well as being poorly constructed

Horses and chaldron waggons near Ryton, Tyne & Wear. (British Library Collection)

and even less well maintained, the pre-eighteenth-century roads were dangerous places. The threat of armed robbery by the notorious highwayman was ever present; even, perhaps particularly, wealthy and well-protected travellers were at risk. The late seventeenth-century traveller and explorer Celia Fiennes was nearly one such victim, being ambushed with pistols drawn towards her. Fortunately Fiennes and her party were sufficiently close to the town of Whitchurch in Shropshire to gallop to safety. Apparently highwaymen really did demand the passengers' money and treasured possessions with the immortal phrases, 'Stand and deliver!' and, 'Your money or your life!' They operated on the main routes under cover of heath and woodland, but if caught, were sentenced to the gallows or, at the very least, a free passage to Van Diemen's Land. Once the majority of roads were turnpiked and gates and tolls more widely introduced to pay for their upkeep, the highwayman's getaway was thwarted. The last case of a highway robbery was reported in 1831.

In many places a ready-made alternative to the poor roads was water – our seas and rivers, but only later to be joined by the network of canals. It was the accessibility of the rivers Tyne and Wear, and thus through to the North Sea, that enabled the north-east of England to become the first area to export and transport large amounts of coal to other places. Whilst coal was being mined in many parts of the country, the 'coal trade' became associated with that area. This gave rise to the phrase 'Coals to

Newcastle', gently mocking the idea of taking a resource back to an area which had plenty of its own.

However, the Industrial Revolution's effect on the transportation system was going to change all that. With the development of factories and the consequent mechanisation of production, there was a huge need for a transportation system which not only supplied the raw materials and fuel to the factories, but provided a route for the finished goods to be distributed around the country, or perhaps worldwide.

2

Early History

Although there is clear evidence that wheeled trucks with various forms of guidance had been used by miners underground in mainland Europe for centuries before 1600 – what is thought to be a 'railway' of Roman origin has been discovered in a gold mine in Portugal – it was around that time that the use of waggons running overland on wooden rails developed in England. Recent archaeological findings have confirmed that in the sixteenth century, the continental 'hund' system was used in Britain, at the Mines Royal Museum at Caldbeck near Keswick, in Cumbria, but was only in operation underground. This was effectively simple haulage of small mine tubs with roller wheels on flat board rails steered by a central guide pin in the manner of a Scalextric track. It was known as a 'hund' from the German word for dog as the noise the wheels made apparently sounded like a dog barking. The first recognisable form of a smooth and elevated course was the laying down of planks of wood – these were generally about 6ft long, 5–6in in width and of a constant depth. Sleepers were placed horizontally at 2ft intervals so each 'rail' reached across three sleepers. The space between sleepers was then filled with ashes or small stones in order to create a level surface.

So whilst it is entirely possible that such 'railways' might in places have led out of mines to some sort of land or river-based collection or distribution point, documentary evidence is lacking. The earliest possible reference to an 'open air' railway comes from the November 1931 edition of the *Railway Magazine* which reported mention of a laid log track near Barnard Castle in Durham in a will of 1555. It is also known that in some collieries, by the late sixteenth century, wooden rails, known as tilted rails

An example of an underground quarry tramway at Winspit Quarry on Purbeck in Dorset, at one time also used as a film location for *Dr Who*! (Richard Lewis)

were permitting the operation of waggons with flanged wheels, thus clearly differentiating them from standard 'road-based' carts.

Progress was clearly being made, as the first generally accepted documented surface tramroad was opened at Wollaton in Nottinghamshire in 1604. Built by the splendidly named Huntingdon Beaumont, this line linked pits at Strelley with a 'yard' at Wollaton Lane, where the coal presumably continued its onward journey by road. A possible rival is a very early railway at Prescot on Merseyside, again running from a pit – in this case near Prescot Hall – for about half a mile to Fall Lane where, again, one presumes a suitable road was available to take the materials to where they were needed. A line at Broseley in Shropshire was only slightly later.

In these early days little was known about how to build or design a track or to make adequate provision for gradients. It is recorded that, around 1630, the aforementioned Mr Beaumont visited the colliery districts of the north east, to offer his services in improving the track. Until then much of the coal was taken from the mines in bags on horses' backs and in horse-drawn carts along flagstone ways to boats moored at staithes alongside the rivers Tyne and Wear. After a few years Beaumont was apparently practically bankrupt but his input had improved many waggonways to the extent that horses could pull more waggons (hooked together) and could travel faster. One assumes that his role was to lay out a track at a gradient suitable for loaded waggons to travel downhill at a controlled velocity, whilst also being manageable for bringing back the empties. Details of how this might have been achieved are discussed in later chapters. Gradually, earthworks such as cuttings and embankments were built to achieve a more level route, but in 1725 a major new development was ready to take centre stage.

The Causey Arch, on the Tanfield Railway in Northumberland, was the first major piece of civil engineering of its type since Roman times. It should be noted that it precedes anything of similar size on our canals. An 1812 description of the bridge from Akenhead's *Picture of Newcastle Upon Tyne* sets the scene well:

> Over the deep and Romantic Dell of Cawsey Burne near Tanfield Arch built by the Grand Allies to form a level for the passage of coal waggons. The span of the arch is 103 feet; it springs from abutments about nine feet high and, being semicircular, the entire elevation is about sixty feet. It Cost £12,000.

Preserved flat-bottomed, low-sided waggon. (Author)

Its architect was Ralph Wood, a common mason, who having built a former arch of wood, that fell for want of weight, committed suicide from a dread of this beautiful structure experiencing the same fate. It is at present neglected and falling into ruins.

It is a shame Ralph Wood did not have more faith in his structure as the arch still stands, now preserved as a scheduled ancient monument, and is discussed further in Chapter 7. As an aside, it may be noted that the Romans never developed the skill of building skew bridges; all their arches are perpendicular to whatever it was they were crossing. Skew bridges were therefore a significant development and progression of civil engineering skills.

Tramroads were not always popular – perhaps for the reason that any labour-saving device has the potential to put men out of work. In places major disruption was caused by 'Luddite' type action; an example being on the Middleton Railway at Leeds Pottery where, on 31 December 1812, stone and iron were placed on the line in order to cause damage to a train. Much earlier in 1698 a colliery railway at Neath in South Wales was condemned after an eight-year existence as 'a nuisance' by a Grand Jury in Cardiff, who ordered the tracks to be pulled up; though it is not entirely clear who was the sufferer of the said nuisance. In 1776 a plate-way track was laid to form a coal line at the Duke of Norfolk's colliery close to Sheffield and was called a cast-iron tramway. For reasons unknown, the colliery workers fiercely resented the new track, tore it up and started a riot. The man who had laid the line, a certain John Curr, fled to a nearby wood and was forced to hide there for three days and three nights.

On the other hand, the use of rails reduced the heavy physical demands on many workers and the same John Curr was celebrated in a 1776 verse by a Geordie poet named Thomas Wilson:

> God Bless the man wi' peace and plenty
> That first invented metal plates.
> Draw out his years to five times twenty
> Then slide him through the heavenly gates

Whilst tramways were being gradually developed and improved in the north east of England, elsewhere another form of transport was to take precedence for a while. Navigable rivers were valuable conduits of transport and evidence of statutory regulation of their use dates back to the setting up of the River Lea authority in 1424. The 1500s saw the construction of the Exeter Canal, built to bypass a number of weirs built across the River

Exe which had blocked navigation into the city and affected local trade for over 200 years. By the 1660s, a number of Acts of Parliament were being passed to affect 'improvements' to rivers to allow the passage of boats – such improvements continued so as to allow larger and larger vessels to reach towns and cities further upstream. These early acts included works on the Worcestershire Stour, the Medway and the Itchen.

Ironically, it was the industrial areas of Lancashire and the Midlands which were least well served by the river network. The answer was to bring the rivers to them with the construction of man-made water channels, known as canals. One of the first of these new canals was the Sankey Brook Navigation which opened in 1757, linking the coalfields of the St Helens area of Lancashire to the city of Liverpool and the River Mersey. It was originally intended to straighten the existing brook; however, it proved much more practical to build a separate artificial cut running beside it. The construction of more canals followed, particularly as the price of coal supplied through them undercut the opposition. The Bridgewater Canal,

Stone blocks on the Treffry Railway, adjacent to the Par Canal, Cornwall. (Richard Lewis)

linking Runcorn, Leigh and Manchester was completed by 1761. This involved the construction of an aqueduct over the River Irwell – the first of its kind. This aqueduct was unfortunately destroyed in the 1890s, when it was forced to make way for the construction of the Manchester Ship Canal.

The age of the canal had truly arrived, and the closing decades of the eighteenth century saw the canal network expanding so that cities, industrial areas and ports were linked through a system of waterways, serving the demands of the new industrialised nation.

By 1830 the country had over 4,000 miles of navigable waterways, and this, together with the road network, provided the backbone of the inland transportation system. So our 'second generation' of tramroads was largely built to serve and act as an extension to the canal system.

Preserved section of plateway from the Surrey Iron Railway. As discussed later, the Surrey Iron Railway's claim to be the first public railway in the world has now been challenged. (Leslie Oppitz Collection)

The development of 'canal based' tramways was largely powered by economics – if there was coal, stone or other merchandise to be sourced but a canal was not affordable, then a tramway might be considered. In many cases this was topographical; in some places no canal could be built without a huge expenditure on locks (which would slow down the traffic anyway) or major earthworks, whereas a gradually and continuously descending tramroad, using much less land, might be considerably easier and cheaper to build. By the early 1800s, past the days of great profits for navigations during the 'Canal Mania' period, it simply became cheaper to construct a tramroad – indeed the Radstock extension of the Somerset Coal Canal, which included a tunnel at Wellow, was built as a canal but never held water, a tramway being laid on its bed instead. In places such as the Marple flight on the Peak Forest Canal and at Caen Hill near Devizes on the Kennet & Avon Canal, a tramway was laid on a temporary basis whilst funds were sought to construct the locks required to link two parts of the canal. One notable exception to this 'co-operation' was the Surrey Iron Railway, which was effectively a direct competitor to the slightly later Croydon Canal with which it shared a roughly parallel route. In his *Lost Canals of Great Britain*, Ronald Russell imagined the tramroad horses and canal nags neighing to each other across the fields as they hauled their loads.

Before going on to discuss the construction and operation of our tramroads, it is worth spending a little time discussing the terminology, which is rather more confusing than might be imagined. Firstly, the term 'tram': it is erroneously thought by some that 'tram' derives from the surname of Benjamin Outram, constructor of many of the major routes of the late eighteenth and early nineteenth centuries. However, it is clear that the term was in use before Outram gained any fame, if not before his birth. The word 'tram' or similar may be seen in Swedish – *trum* meaning a log – or in Lower German where *traam* is a term for a beam. The same *traam* is a term for a wooden frame in Norwegian and, closer to home, *dram* has a similar meaning in Welsh. This leads on to the use of the term *dramway* in Welsh, which migrated across the River Severn to become the informal name of the Avon & Gloucestershire Railway.

Should our lines be termed railway or tramway or tramroad? Our early lines have been rather pushed out in terminology terms by later and better-known types of line. Many of our early routes were known as railways, and a number of later ones as tramways. However, the word 'railway' has naturally become associated with more modern locomotive-carrying tracks, and tramway has come to be associated with urban or suburban electric streetcar lines. This rather leaves us just with tramroad as an identifying term, though clearly not the one commonly used in many places. In the north east of England 'waggonway' was used instead, but this also gained use as a term for later standard gauge mineral lines in the locality which were never horse drawn. Plateway has a more specific meaning which we shall explore in the next chapter. It should also be noted that a number of minor passenger lines that were constructed under the auspices of the 1896 Light Railway Act such as at Wantage in Oxfordshire and the Rye and Camber line in Sussex also became known as tramways.

3

Construction

The story of the development of methods of construction is a long and complex one. First we can safely state that our seventeenth-century lines had very little in the way of civil engineering works, so we can move straightaway on to discussion of the actual rails. Although the construction details of the very earliest lines are unrecorded, the early examples at Wollaton and Broseley built in the early 1600s are known to have had flanged wheels running on wooden beams or edge rails. Wear and tear on the wooden rails, together with the rotting action of a damp environment ensured that such rails never lasted long. None of the original wooden rails have survived – in any case they were never intended to last and those lines that endured and prospered had to replace their rails at regular intervals – but there are a few lengths from underground workings that were fortunate to find themselves left untouched in a dry environment preserved in local museums.

In 1676 tramways consisted of rails of timber, laid, as a contemporary account describes, 'from the colliery to the river exactly straight and

Stone sleeper block with nail holes from the Middleton Railway, Leeds. (Author)

parallel, whereby the carriage was so easy that one horse would draw down four or five chaldron [a four-sided wooden waggon of bucket design; the name derives from 'cauldron'] of coals'. The rails originally were formed of oak, and were connected by sills or cross timbers of the same material pinned together with oak 'nails'. Ash was sometimes used as an alternative, though later it was discovered that beech was the wood most resistant to decay and to general wear and tear.

At some unrecorded stage an additional or wearing rail, which could be easily renewed when worn, was placed above the supporting rail, and it became possible to cover the cross pieces or sleepers with earth to protect them from the horses' feet. Plates 2in wide by ½in thick were used and 1767 saw the introduction of cast-iron rails.

Cast iron was thought to have been first developed in 1767 by the Coalbrookdale Iron Company, but it has also been suggested that such rails were being made at Hunslet Carr in Leeds for the Middleton Railway prior to its opening in 1758. The iron rails were cast in lengths of 5ft and formed with three holes, through which they were fastened to the oak rails. These bars or rails were about 2in wide by ½in thick, and were fastened to the wood rails by wrought-iron spikes. But the iron bars, not being stiff enough, bent considerably when the trucks were loaded, and the resistance was reduced, though slightly below that of a well-constructed double wooden tramway.

These early rails also suffered from brittleness which was only overcome by the use of smaller waggons or multiple axles which distributed the weight more evenly. At Prior Park in Bath in 1730 Ralph Allen used edge rails with very deep cast-iron flanges on the rails. This was regarded as a particular well-engineered and constructed line for its time. The tramway was developed into the railway by the employment of cast-iron flange rails to replace the wooden rails; the continuous flange or ledge on their inner edge kept the wheels on the track. The Middleton Railway was converted to a form of rack-rail locomotive use as early as 1812 but later reverted back to horse propulsion for many years.

Rudimentary construction of pointwork on the Severn & Wye Railway in the Forest of Dean. (Bertram Baxter Collection)

PLATEWAYS

For a time from the mid-1700s to the early 1800s some waggonways were built using an L-shaped iron rail system and plain flanged, normal, cart wheels. This style of line became known as a plateway. The first known example is one built near Whitehaven in Cumbria around 1738. Perhaps the most significant of the L-plate systems was England's first public railway, the Surrey Iron Railway of 1803 and sections of track from that line have fortunately survived to be preserved. A similar set-up was utilised on the Little Eaton Gangway in Derbyshire shortly afterwards.

Around the 1830s, some plateways began to use cast-iron chairs on top of the sleepers to hold the rails in place laterally. This consisted of iron rails laid on wooden sleepers. The name comes from the plate-like form from which the rail were cast and this led onto the term 'platelayer', which is still used today for someone who is responsible for checking and maintaining track.

Around 1750, wooden wheels began to be replaced by the introduction of cast-iron wheels which allowed the capacity of a waggon to be increased from 17cwt to 42cwt, but in turn put more pressure on the rails. As noted above, plates or rails were laid with an inner flange to give an L-shaped cross section so that waggons with plain (ordinary) wheels would stay on the track. However, despite some merits to the system when routes were operating on a small scale with horse haulage, as the railway era with steam locomotives expanded the L-rail system was seen as a 'blind alley' and it gradually faded into disuse.

Returning to eighteenth-century iron rails; these were generally cast in 3ft lengths, weighing 47–50lb and had square holes at each end for nailing them to stone sleeper blocks. It is these stone sleeper blocks that survive on many of the old routes, often with holes still visible where the nails were hammered in. A problem that soon became apparent was that the rail was liable to be covered with dust. Therefore, in 1789, Jessop laid down at Loughborough cast-iron 'edge rails', raised above the ground so as to allow a flanged cast-iron wheel to run on them. This appears to have been the first system of rails laid on cast-iron chairs and on sleepers. The rails were pinned or bolted into the chairs. Around the same time some lines such as the Clydach Tramway experimented with metal sleepers, but quickly reverted to the more usual stone type.

Given the clear limitations of cast-iron rails, further development was clearly needed. A wrought-iron rail was patented by Birkenshaw in 1820, known informally as the 'fish-belly' rail due to its cross-sectional shape. It was similar in form and mode of support to Jessop's rail, but was rolled

Pointwork at Morwellham Quay, near Tavistock, Devon. (Richard Lewis).

in continuous lengths, embracing a number of spans, with stiffening ledges of flanges on the under side. This form of rail was adapted to be the forerunner of the rails we still see today. It was first used on the Tindale Fell (Lord Carlisle's) Railway in Cumbria and soon afterwards on the 4ft 6in gauge Monkland & Kirkintilloch Railway. It weighed 33lb per yard, and was laid in cast-iron chairs, spiked down to square or stone blocks around 3ft apart. The edge rail and the flanged wheel remain to this day the basis of the whole system of a railway. These rails met with the approval of

George Stephenson who soon afterwards recommended their use to the committee of the Stockton & Darlington Railway.

Moving on to the stone sleeper blocks; it first needs to be said that cross sleepers were largely unsuitable for horses and that the space between the rails was either cobbled or some form of firm surface. The stone sleeper blocks were generally formed of the local stone, the same as the railway actually carried. Granite blocks can be found on the Plymouth & Dartmoor Railway in Devon, and the nearby Haytor Granite Tramway took this one stage further by constructing 'granite rails' for the waggons to run on.

CIVIL ENGINEERING

In an early reference to the construction of the Tanfield Railway in 1721 it was noted that the:

> ... ground must be made as level as possible without narrow (sharp) turnings, and pieces of hard timber or wood called sleepers [NB the term was used erroneously here] must be fixed in the ground and raised some inches from the ground so waggons can use it but not carts.

A further observation was provided by Benjamin Outram:

> If such trade be both ways in nearly equal quantities a line as nearly horizontal (level) as possible should be chosen. If the trade is all in one direction – as generally the case between mines (or quarries) and navigations what is required is one with a gentle descent such as shall not make it greater labour for the horses to haul the loaded waggons down than the empty ones back.

In practice this meant aiming for a steady gradient of between 1 in 90 and 1 in 180. To achieve this and also to avoid sharp turns or circuitous routes (as were being built on some contemporary canals) it became clear that bridges, embankments and cuttings would sometimes be required.

Outram was to prove that his practice matched the theory by his construction of the Peak Forest Tramway between quarries at Dove Holes and a basin on the Peak Forest Canal at Bugsworth (Buxworth). This line had an almost constant gradient of 1 in 96 (one eighth of an inch per yard in Outram's terminology) other than on one inclined plane. The Middlebere Tramway on Purbeck in Dorset was similarly constructed but had a lesser gradient of between 1 in 150 and 180 on its descent to Poole Harbour. Jessop's similarly well-engineered Croydon, Merstham & Godstone Iron

Railway used large embankments and a summit cutting to maintain an almost constant 1 in 120 (1in every 10ft) gradient. A formation width of 4 yards was generally considered necessary for a single line with 7 yards for doubled track. The final consideration was the provision of a pathway for the horses between the rails, and for the attendants, to one side, whilst also ensuring that the track was properly drained. This, according to Outram, produced a road that was 'excellent for horses and waggons, moving at a walking pace, providing much cheaper and regular transport than the common road' as well as a serious competitor of the canal for light traffic. It only proved inadequate for heavy locomotives and fast trains at a later date.

It does need noting that the relevant construction skills were not, at first, widely known; the first attempt in 1777 at constructing a tramway to the quarries at Caldon Lowe in Staffordshire was described as 'set out before the true principles of this branch of engineering were well understood, and was very crooked, steep and uneven'. It took three further

Viaduct on the Ruabon Brook Tramway near Ruabon, North Wales. (Author)

attempts before a satisfactory line capable of handling the high volume of traffic required was constructed. The route of the Fordell Railway on the north bank of the River Forth in Scotland, also built in the 1770s, was described as 'making a right-angled turn before crossing a stream on a bridge'. In addition it became clear that civil engineers of the day needed to fully understand the underlying mathematical principles of the design of arches and buttresses, as these were common features of bridges, aqueducts and tunnels. In this respect it was crucial for them to recognise the importance of the work of mathematicians such as Charles Hutton (1737–1823). For civil engineers of the time, the two most important works of Hutton were his *Principles of Bridges* (1772) and *Mathematical Tables* (1785). An original copy of the *Principles of Bridges* is held by Salford University.

Though many such routes were short, perhaps linking a mine or quarry with a canal less than a mile away, others were lengthy undertakings. The Abergavenny to Hereford route was 24 miles long, while the Stockton & Darlington Line, authorised by an Act of Parliament and constructed as a tramroad but operated from the start by locomotives, was 2 or 3 miles further. The Cromford & High Peak Railway, perhaps the best survivor of all, extended to 34 miles but the Hay and Kington lines in Herefordshire were perhaps the longest, with a combined route of 36 miles.

Dial Wood Tunnel on the New Hall Tramway at Flockton near Wakefield in Yorkshire. It possibly opened prior to 1796, which would make it the oldest tramway tunnel in Britain. (John Simmonds)

The title of 'Oldest Railway Tunnel' also remains a subject of some conjecture – Baxter believed that Stodhart Tunnel, of 1796 vintage on the Peak Forest Tramway, was the earliest fully documented tunnel, but it is possible that Dial Wood Tunnel in the Yorkshire village of Flockton may be even older. Lying between Wakefield and Huddersfield, a tunnel of approximately 100 yards, 8ft 6in high, 6ft 5in across and lined with dressed stone was constructed on a tramway which ran from a coal pit at Flockton to the River Calder at Horbury Bridge and opened between 1772 and 1775. However, there are no documentary references or map evidence until 1841. Baxter regarded its existence prior to that of Stodhart as 'likely but unproven'.

Many canal companies built tramways after obtaining their own Act of Parliament. This gave them powers to build tramroads of typically up to 8 miles and particularly in south-east Wales this concession was well used. In some cases, such as the Brinore Tramroad at Talybont on the Monmouthshire & Brecon Canal, a further extension was built by a single landowner, often the owner of the mineral being resourced. These measures were also used in the north east of England, where owners of land between pits and rivers had taken to charging exorbitant fees known as 'wayleaves' effectively taking large chunks of the potential profits of the mine owners.

4

Operating the Tramroads

Tramroads were generally open to all carriers; as a canal or public road operates but not a modern railway. Some lines, such as the Plymouth & Dartmoor Railway at Princetown in Devon, were, however, dominated by one carrier, in this case Johnson Brothers, owners of the huge Cann Quarry. The railway owners therefore had to put into place some system of tolls and regulations to keep some sort of order. The Caldon Low Tramway did not seem to start with any such regulation; not until nearly ten years after opening was a committee resolution passed stating, 'To form sundry regulations respecting the passage of waggons between Froghall and the Limestone quarries at Caldon Low, which they apprehend will be proper to be passed into Bye Laws'.

So what were these regulations? Firstly, the owners of each waggon needed to be identified. The Hay Railway required each waggon to have a metal plate attached, with the owner's name painted on, while the Monmouthshire Company had some form of number system with all drivers having their names and addresses recorded.

Given the limited capacity of the rails to support heavy loads, it was also important to regulate the weight of the waggons, both tare (empty) which could be recorded on the actual truck and also with a full load, which had to be carefully and frequently monitored. On the Hay Railway at Eardisley there was a weighbridge which could be used for both rail and road traffic. Other weighing sometimes took place at a 'machine house', often with a cottage built beside it for the use of an attendant. At the top of Froghall Incline on the Caldon Low Tramroad it was explained that 'each tram of limestone is weighed before it is attached to the great chain and launched onto the plane. Weights ranged between 22 and 30cwt'. As rails became stronger, maximum permitted weights were gradually increased; on the lines controlled by the Monmouthshire Canal Company 40cwt was the maximum permitted in 1799, increasing to 56cwt by 1806 and eventually 70cwt by 1830. The Ashby Tramway and the Walton Summit Plateway also had 40cwt per waggon limits in the early years of the nineteenth century.

Naturally some waggon owners were keen where possible to bend, if not break, the rules set out in bye-laws. On the Severn & Wye line in the Forest of Dean, iron companies apparently attempted to carry upwards of 2 tons of material on one set of wheels. Other regulations were also passed to exclude unauthorised traffic. The Ashby Company provided a penalty for the owner or driver of any carriage on its line 'not properly adapted to the uses thereof', whilst the Monmouthshire in 1830 rather curiously prohibited waggons 'having less than four wheels'.

Little Eaton Wharf on the Little Eaton Gangway. (Author's collection)

The whole concept of a need for some degree of track maintenance took some grasping by the tramway owners. Few records exist, but in 1794 it was ordered by the owners of the Clydach Railroad that 'two active labourers' be employed to keep the track in good order, though as usage increased this was quickly found to be inadequate and by the following year a contractor was engaged and paid the princely sum of £56 per year for the purpose. Similarly on the Little Eaton Gangway in Derbyshire in 1808 one Daniel Smith was given responsibility, together with two workmen, for maintenance but within a year his contract was terminated and replaced by John Peach who felt the need to deploy twelve labourers to carry out the task.

WAGGONS

For the very earliest tramroads a waggon, similar in style to the continental reisen (a low flat-bottomed waggon), is likely to have been the one most commonly used. The body style is also unknown but initially likely to have been derived from the standard coal wains in use at the time. A more box-like structure appears to have been used in Shropshire in places such as Broseley. In common with the wheels and rails, waggons continued to be made from wood until much later in the development of waggonway systems when iron began to be introduced.

As use of such vehicles expanded, many carriers found a hopper body to be the best shape. The chaldron measure for coal used in the north east became a standard measure with waggons built to take that load, the name becoming synonymous for the style of waggon. A modern replica of one of these waggons is on show at the Causey Arch Museum site. This style continued in use in into the 1960s and modern rapid-discharge hopper vehicles used on 'merry go round' workings to power stations are still constructed in that form.

TRAFFIC

Tramways could be operated as double track or single track with passing places. The typical load for a four-wheeled waggon was 2 tons and these were linked together to form a train (in some places termed a 'gang') for the horse to pull. If the line had a gradient a brakeman or boy would control the speed on the descent with the horse required to pull the empties back up the hill. Early illustrations show the 'driver' perched on top of the front waggon holding an enormous lever which he used to operate the brake. Later a device known as a 'long brake' was used, which

Waggons at the foot of a quarry incline at Leckhampton, Gloucester & Cheltenham Railway. (Bertram Baxter collection)

enabled the driver to apply brakes to more than one waggon at a time. This was later developed further into a continuous chain brake.

On plateways, a method of braking known as sledging was described by Outram. This involved putting an iron 'shoe', normally chained to the side of the waggon, under a wheel. Baxter described seeing this primitive system still in operation in the Forest of Dean as late as 1938.

Inclined planes were a feature of tramroads from an early stage. It had originally been believed that lines needed to be exactly level – as canals have to be – and that these were therefore the only practical means of gaining the required height. Many were what were known as 'self-acting', meaning that the weight and force of the loaded waggons travelling downhill was used to pull the empties back up. On Tyneside, the Byker Tramway of 1714 had used an ingenious alternative of zig-zag gradients allowing a gradual descent to the river. This was replaced by a conventional rope haulage system before 1844. The first 'proper' inclined plane is thought possibly to be a 1750s 'balance plane' leading down to the River Severn at Broseley in Shropshire. The other contender is an inclined plane on a 1755 branch off Ralph Allen's 1730 railway which linked quarries at Combe Down above Bath (close to the well-known

Somerset & Dorset Railway Tunnel of that same name) with the River Avon. This plane was built by Allen's clerk of works, Richard Jones, and described by Allen as an 'exceeding good contrivance'.

Where no natural passage of loaded waggons down and empties up existed, steam power from stationary engines was required. The various inclines on the 1830 Cromford & High Peak Tramway were operated in this manner. A horizontal winding drum was powered by the engine, and a short length of cable was attached to the waggons which was wound round the winding drum several times to give the required grip. Self-acting planes were of necessity double track – but most powered ones were also double though originally the Middleton incline on the Cromford & High Peak was single track. In a few places, such as the Caldon Canal Tramroad in Staffordshire and Lord Carlisle's Railway in Cumbria, inclined planes were built with three parallel rails, only dividing into two separate tracks at the actual passing place of the waggons. The Fordell Railway's Colton Incline had an even more curious arrangement, being single track on its lower half and 'three rails' on the upper. Some very long inclines were split into two, with a short level section such as the Pen-Rhiw incline on the Cefn Rhigos Tramway in West Glamorgan between Glyn Neath and Abernant. On Lord Elgin's tramway at Dunfermline in Scotland, the two inclines were connected by short sections of track graded in opposite directions, so that the waggons in both directions would run from the head of one plane to the foot of the other.

HAULAGE

Although horses were almost always the haulage of choice, there were occasions when equine availability was limited and alternatives had to be sought. It has been suggested that in times of war large numbers of horses were 'conscripted', leading to a shortage at home, but this would presumably have been only temporary, with no doubt a healthy profit being made by the breeders. In 1803 it was reported that Pickfords, already well established as both a road and canal-based carrier, had offered the government the loan of 400 horses to support the war effort of the time. When other creatures were used to haul barges on the canals of the West Midlands, they were known collectively as 'animals'. Both ponies and mules were used on the Severn & Wye line in the Forest of Dean in the early days. Oxen were tried on the Wylam route north of the River Tyne in 1811, and may also have been used in Leicestershire on the Ashby to Ticknall line, as a company bye-law of 1804 refers to 'Horses or Cattle'.

Horse and waggon on Fordell Railway, near Dunfermline, Scotland. (Bertram Baxter collection)

Although a horse can clearly reach a quite appreciable trotting speed, especially on a gravelled or cobbled path, this was discouraged by most tramway companies. The Hay Railway enforced a walking pace by prohibiting the driver from riding on the horse at all, while the Monmouthshire Company enforced a speed limit of just 4mph, increasing to a heady 5mph by 1832. The Severn & Wye Railway forbade the driver 'taking any tram down any of the branches faster than a horse can walk'.

USE OF THE LINE

Although the penalties for overloading a waggon fell on the owner, responsibility for any mistakes en route fell firmly on the shoulders of the driver. Firstly he had to ensure the load did not overhang the waggon and potentially damage a bridge or a boundary fence. If there was a derailment, he had to get everything back on track – the Hay Railway allowed just fifteen minutes for this – or else the waggons had to be cleared from the track altogether. Both the Lancaster and Monmouthshire

Surviving pointwork on the Treffry Railway, near Par, Cornwall. (Chris McFarlane)

Companies required the driver to carry some form of 'jack' for raising the wheels back onto the track and did not permit the use of the horse to 'drag' the waggon back into place. The driver of the waggons was also responsible for carrying the 'waybill', the signed account of the quantity and description of the goods being carried, ready to give to the toll collector. On edge railways it was possible for road carts to use the line, without fee or permission and in places gates with locks had to be positioned to prevent this.

PASSENGER CARRIAGE

Publicly advertised passenger services were few; probably the best known and successful was the first – the Swansea to Mumbles Line (see p.87) – which commenced operation in 1807, though the Edinburgh &

Dalkeith Line (see p.125) was hauling 300,000 passengers per year shortly before conversion to locomotive haulage. The Cromford & High Peak Railway offered a service – operated by a licence given to an outside firm – from Cromford to Whaley Bridge (where means of conveyance onwards to Manchester was, rather curiously, 'presumed') which started in 1833. This consisted simply of a single carriage pulled by a single horse. By the 1850s, when facing competition from 'locomotive hauled' lines, the service was summer only. By the 1860s passengers were very few, one visiting inspector finding just two passengers on one occasion in 1862, but somehow, perhaps simply due to the loss of face and prestige that closure implied, the service struggled on until 1876 when it was quietly stopped. In Cornwall Sunday School parties were carried free of charge by the Pentewan Railway in china clay waggons to Pentewan Harbour.

Also worthy of mention were the 'fly' or 'dandy' horse-drawn passenger services on what were otherwise conventional locomotive-hauled railways. There were two well-known examples in Cumbria – the Carlisle to Port Carlisle service and the Brampton Town to Brampton Junction line (see p.122) – to this day the route is known as the 'dandy' line.

'Dandy Car' with horse at Port Carlisle station.

5

The Beginning of the End

Perhaps somewhat perversely, we shall start this chapter with what might be termed 'the end of the beginning'. As the development of bigger and bigger industrial sites took place, the demands on the transport infrastructure serving them became more difficult to manage. For example, by 1786 the huge Ravenhead Plate Glass and Smelting works in St Helens on Merseyside were consuming well over 700 tons of coal per week. Earlier we have discussed the close link between the canals and many of our tramways – but the limitations of canals as a reliable mode of transport were gradually becoming clear. Delays in traffic were frequent, with canals frozen up and impassable for long periods in the winter months when supplies were most needed. Conversely, water shortages during prolonged periods of dry weather could also shut down stretches of canal (and of course both these situations can cause similar problems to this day). There was also much dissatisfaction with the standard of canal maintenance, with water leaking away at locks and landslips on embankments and cuttings not being promptly made good.

It is worth pausing for a while here to briefly review the life and times of some of the most notable civil engineers associated with our tramroads. Benjamin Outram was born in Derbyshire in 1764 into a wealthy family, his father Joseph being an ironmaster and a surveyor. Clearly growing up in an engineering environment was an advantage, as by 1789 he was working with the experienced William Jessop on the design of the Cromford Canal, including the 2,966-yard Butterley Tunnel. His first tramroad is thought to be a line slightly over a mile in length, built to carry limestone from quarries at Crich to Bullbridge Wharf on the Cromford Canal for use by his works. He moved on in 1795 to construct the Little Eaton Gangway, a well-engineered line 5 miles in length from the Little Eaton arm of the Derby Canal to the Drury Low Colliery at Denby. By the late 1790s Outram was much in demand and a very busy man, working on tramways such as the Peak Forest, the survey and construction of Standedge Tunnel on the Huddersfield Narrow Canal and at the same time overseeing the development of his own ironworks, later to become the Butterley Company. It was therefore something of a surprise to his friends that he found time to get married in 1800, becoming betrothed to Margaret Anderson, daughter of a well-known Scottish scientist. Outram was clearly not a man to cross; his wife wrote some years after his death that 'Outram was hasty in his temper, feeling his own superiority over others. Accustomed to command, he had little toleration for stupidity and slowness, and none for meanness or littleness of any kind.' By 1800 Outram, clear in his mind of the value of tramroads, was promoting the possibilities of a fully interconnecting national network linking together what at its height was about 1,500 miles of track, ideally using his preferred 4ft 2in gauge; this was later supported by a number of other authors including R.L. Edgeworth, who advocated the laying of tracks alongside the main roads of the day.

But by 1820 it was becoming clear that locomotive haulage would be the future. Returning to Outram, still busy, he began to spread his wings south and west, working on potential tramway routes for the Brecknock & Abergavenny Company and advising on a possible route from the Severn to the Wye. All this was to end suddenly in 1805 when, on a visit to London, Outram suffered a stroke and sadly died at the age of just forty-one.

Let us next consider George Overton. Born ten years after Outram in January 1775, by the age of just nineteen Overton was working with the aforementioned John Curr, the man sometimes credited with the invention of the plate rail. Moving to the Merthyr area in the late 1790s, Overton found work as a mining engineer and developed sufficient reputation to be entrusted with the survey and engineering of a number of tramways including the Sirhowy and the Brinore lines. Indeed George Overton could in some ways be considered Outram's equivalent in South Wales, though his work was spread over a longer period of time, right through to the days of decline in tramroad building. However, Overton's status as a top civil engineer was to suffer a major blow when he was summarily replaced by George Stephenson as engineer to the Stockton & Darlington Railway in a manner described later.

Richard Trevithick was a Cornish inventor who had developed a number of different types of engines using high-pressure steam. In 1802, Trevithick built one of his high pressure steam engines to drive a hammer at the Pen-y-Darren Ironworks in Merthyr Tydfil. With the assistance of Rees Jones, an employee of the ironworks and under the supervision of Samuel Homfray, the proprietor, he mounted the engine on wheels and turned it into a locomotive. However, his reputation suffered when, in 1803, one of his stationary pumping engines in use at Greenwich exploded, killing four men. However, in the same year Trevithick sold the patents for his locomotives to Samuel Homfray. Homfray was so impressed with Trevithick's locomotive that he made a bet with another ironmaster, Richard Crawshay, for 500 guineas that Trevithick's steam locomotive could haul 10 tons of iron along the local (Penydarren) tramroad to Abercynon. The first private locomotive trial took place on 13 February 1804, then eight days later on the 21 February 1804 a load of 10 tons of 'bar iron' was hauled, apparently with about seventy men also riding on the waggons, taking just over four hours to complete the journey. We have seen in previous chapters how developments in material and management of the track had enabled heavier and heavier loads of waggons to travel upon them, but this was still the main obstacle to early locomotive operation; it was not the engine that failed but the cast-iron tram plates that were not strong enough to support the weight of the engine.

After Trevithick, the next known attempt at locomotive haulage took place in August 1812 on the Middleton Railway near Leeds. Matthew Murray built two locomotives which used the rack railway system, and apparently operated in this manner for around thirty years. The locomotives weighed 5 tons and could haul a load of 94 tons at a typical walking pace of 3½mph, quite some achievement. Rack railways were not developed further in Britain; they did, however, prove useful and popular in more hilly countries such as Switzerland, where the technology developed further; Britain's only modern rack railway, on Snowdon, uses a modified version of such a system.

At around the same time William Hedley, manager of the Wylam Colliery and Plateway on the north bank of the River Tyne, was building locomotives. At least four were tried on his 5ft gauge plateway, which had a switchback gradient and was thus difficult for horses to operate effectively. His early efforts again proved too heavy for the lightly built track, but in 1815 he rebuilt one so that the load was shared by two separate four-wheeled bogies. This enabled the engine, known as *Puffing Billy*, to operate quite effectively for some years, but when the line was reconstructed as an edge railway the engine reverted to a single bogie.

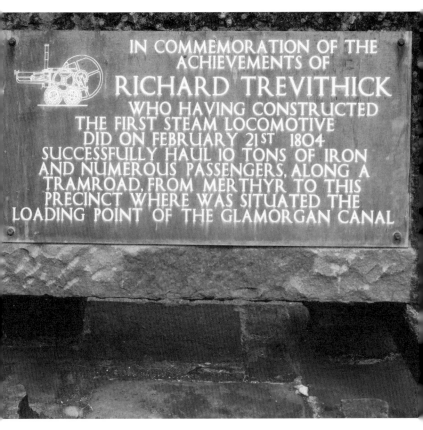

Plaque outside Abercynon fire station commemorating the first successful locomotive haulage along the Penydarren Tramway. (Author)

This brings us on to George Stephenson, though here we will limit our discussion to events up to the opening of the Stockton & Darlington Railway. With the help of his manager from Killingworth Colliery, Nicholas Wood, Stephenson designed his first locomotive in 1814, a travelling engine designed for hauling coal on the Killingworth Waggonway, and named *Blücher* after a Prussian General of that name. It was constructed in the colliery workshop behind Stephenson's home, Dial Cottage, near Killingworth, in what is now a suburb of Newcastle upon Tyne. This locomotive could haul 30 tons of coal up a slight gradient at 4mph and was the first successful flanged-wheel adhesion locomotive: its traction depended only on the contact between its flanged wheels and the rail. Altogether, Stephenson is said to have produced sixteen locomotives at

Killingworth, although no convincing list of the existence and usage of them all has ever been produced. Of those that have been identified most were built for use at Killingworth itself or for the Hetton Colliery Railway, an 8-mile line from Hetton Colliery to Sunderland completed in 1820. This line used a combination of gravity on downward inclines and locomotives for level and upward stretches, making it the first railway to need no animal power. Another of Stephenson's creations was a six-wheeled locomotive built for the Kilmarnock & Troon Railway in 1817 but soon withdrawn from service because of damage it caused to the cast-iron rails. A further locomotive was supplied to Scott's Pit railroad at Llansamlet near Swansea in 1819 but it too was soon withdrawn, apparently because it was under-boilered and yet again because of damage to the track. The noted transport historian L.T.C. Rolt later described how Stephenson managed to solve the problem caused by the weight of the engine upon these primitive rails. He experimented with a 'steam spring' (to 'cushion'

Tramway points at Pentewan Harbour, Cornwall. (Richard Lewis)

the weight using steam pressure), but soon followed the new practice of distributing weight by utilising a greater number of wheels and axles.

Conceived by a wealthy local wool merchant named Edward Pease, the Stockton & Darlington Railway was originally engineered by George Overton and authorised by Parliament in 1821; it was initially intended to be an ordinary horse-drawn plateway, indeed locomotive haulage was specifically ruled out in the original Act. However, Stephenson persuaded Pease on the day that the Act received royal assent to allow him to resurvey the route and work it, at least partly, by steam. Accordingly, a new Act of Parliament was obtained approving Stephenson's changes to the route, and a clause added to permit the use of 'loco-motive or moveable engines'. This latter clause narrowly escaped being struck out of the bill because of officials not understanding the meaning. The bill also included provisions for transporting passengers although, at the time, they were regarded as little more than a sideline.

It might have been expected that once steam had proved its worth that horse power might fade away quickly, but in some places this was not to prove the case. Tramroads that opened after 1830 included the Cromford & High Peak Railway and the Festiniog Railway in Wales, which opened in 1836, but was not converted to locomotive haulage until 1863. The Storeton Tramway on the Wirral opened in 1837, using stone blocks bought second hand from the Liverpool & Manchester Line; whilst the Treffry Railway in Cornwall did not open for business until 1847. Which tramroad was the very last to be constructed is debatable; one candidate is the colliery branch network associated with the Poynton Tramway in north-east Cheshire. The last 'new venture' use of a tramroad might well have been the 1881 reopening of the lower part of the Avon & Gloucester Railway from California Colliery at Willsbridge, east of Bristol, down to the River Avon at Keynsham, which operated profitably enough until the colliery was closed by a flood in 1904.

The First World War led to a temporary reprieve in places; demands for goods such as limestone became almost limitless during wartime, and this certainly kept lines such as the Caldon Low and Peak Forest Tramroads in business until around 1920. Others to survive into the twentieth century included the aforementioned Little Eaton Gangway (closed 1908), the Belvoir Castle Railway (not used after 1918), whilst minor branches of the former Severn & Wye Railway in the Forest of Dean (see p.102) remained horse drawn into the 1930s. However, the Nantlle line (see p.112), helped by its unusual 'betwixt and between' 3ft 6in gauge, remained horse drawn into the British Railways era and into the 1960s; there were simply no suitable locomotives available to replace the trusty steeds.

Horses and waggon on the Belvoir Castle Railway, Lincolnshire. Note the wooden stake at the back of the waggon used for braking. (Author's collection)

Cut and cover tunnel on the Nantlle Railway, Gwynedd. (Richard Lewis)

So what happened to the tramroads and the companies that ran them? Some were turned over to locomotive haulage, becoming an integral part of the nineteenth-century rail network – indeed on one or two former routes such as the Kilmarnock & Troon line such a converted railway is still in operation. The Middleton Railway – always just that distance apart in operation from other tramroads – remains in operation as a preserved line, though it tends these days to dwell somewhat more on its locomotive haulage era than its eighteenth-century origins.

Many lines of course simply ceased to operate when the mine or quarry they served closed – they no longer had a purpose. A few common carriers such as the Brinore Tramroad never formally ceased to trade either, waggons just gradually stopped running and in this case the company was never wound up either – it limped along for over twenty-five years after the last tram ran in the 1860s – holding a committee meeting in 1890 which was adjourned but never reconvened, and thus the line just faded away. But that 'fading away' in a way helped preserve the Brinore (see p 94) in the form it is today – there was no one trying to sell or convert the line, no one to buy the line from – which leads us gently into starting to look at what remains of our tramroads today.

1. Trackbed showing the line's distinctive 'diamond'-shaped sleeper blocks, Silkstone Railway. (Author)

2. The Llangattock tramway runs along a spectacular ledge for much of its route. (Richard Lewis collection)

3. Replica trackbed, incline and tunnel at Cromford & High Peak Railway. (Author)

4. Clearly defined trackbed of Congleton Railway. (Author)

5. Tree-lined section of Storeton Tramway. (Howard Harrison)

6. Tramway bridge at Lambley Colliery, Lord Carlisle's Railway. (Author)

7. A view inside Britain's longest tramway tunnel at Pwll Du. (Philip Earnshaw)

8. Causey Arch from river level. (Author)

6

Exploring Tramroads

There are two main aims of this chapter – first to discuss how to find and explore what remains of the former tramways and secondly to describe some surviving features and structures which do not feature in the following chapter.

So let us start at the beginning – you are aware that a tramroad once ran through a particular location and wish to trace any remains – what might you find? Firstly it is not out of the question that you might find nothing left at all. This could be either because the route has been built upon or just as likely ploughed away or obliterated. Ronald Russell, in his *Lost Canals & Waterways of Britain* wrote of the Croydon Canal: 'exploring the heavily built up area between New Cross and Croydon in search of the remains of a canal which was obliterated over 140 years ago is an activity that will appeal to few' and unfortunately more than a few tramroads have suffered a similar fate.

With that thought firmly in the back of your mind, let us imagine trying to work out where our tramway might be. An up-to-date map is a good starting point; particularly one from the 1:25000 Explorer series. However, whilst any 'on the ground' remains of former 'railways' will be marked, many tramways are not, unless they form some part of a public right of way. So our would-be explorer sometimes has to start with the most basic information – where did the tramroad start and where did it terminate – and then try to work out a possible route. In some areas it is possible to obtain copies of older maps – a local library might be able to help or the 'Godfrey' series of old (generally early twentieth century) Ordnance

Tiny tramway bridge at Pontcysyllte basin on the Llangollen Canal. (Author)

Survey maps might provide some guidance to what was in place at the tail end of the eighteenth century. In certain counties, such as Cheshire, CDs are available with very large-scale maps of the entire county from a somewhat earlier period such as the mid-nineteenth century, which can help considerably if available. Unfortunately even maps over 100 years old often completely fail to show the course or formation of a tramroad once it ceased to operate. If you can get hold of an old map of the area you are interested in and which shows the line in situ alongside a more modern guide you may find it possible to start to establish the tramroad's route. Street maps can also be useful, particularly if they indicate a relevant name; perhaps a Wharf Street, a 'Tramway Road' or an 'Old Tram Road' or as in Hirwaun in Wales, a road named simply 'Tramway'.

 If we imagine our tramroad running from some remote quarry down to a roadside or canal-side wharf, it is at the latter location we can expect to find more in the way of surviving buildings, so if our tramway started from a wharf on a canal that may be a good starting point – unless, that is,

Sleeper blocks at Stratford-upon-Avon Basin (Stratford & Moreton Railway), 1932. All traces were swept away shortly afterwards. (Bertram Baxter collection)

the canal has itself closed. There might perhaps be some sort of plaque or information board giving details of the tramroad, what it carried and its dates of use. Or perhaps there might be a replica waggon on a set of rails, as can be seen now outside the Gloucester Docks buildings commemorating the Gloucester & Cheltenham Railway.

Of routes where most of the formation survives, a number owe their continued existence to having been incorporated as public rights of way. If it was accepted that any competent person could obtain and operate one or more waggons, then that same person could obviously walk up and down the track leading his horse. In the early days of tramways, it was apparently also not uncommon for local people to use them as short cuts between communities, and it would appear that public rights of way evolved alongside the rails. When the lines closed, the rights of way remained. There is a surprising archive photograph from Pembrokeshire which shows a lady returning from market, basket in arm, walking along

Original rail from the Gloucester & Cheltenham Railway with replica waggons at Gloucester Docks together with plaque. (Author)

THE PORT OF GLOUCESTER

THE GLOUCESTER AND CHELTENHAM TRAMROAD (1811 — 1861)

THROUGH THIS GATEWAY, THE NINE MILE LONG TRAMROAD ENTERED THE DOCKS. WAGONS CARRYING GOODS AND MINERALS WERE PULLED BY HORSES ALONG CAST—IRON RAILS HAVING A GAUGE OF 3 FT. 6 IN. (1·1M). IT WAS THE FIRST RAILWAY IN THE COUNTY AUTHORISED BY ACT OF PARLIAMENT. THE STEAM LOCOMOTIVE ROYAL WILLIAM WAS TRIED IN 1831 OR 1832 BUT ITS WEIGHT BROKE THE RAILS.

THIS PLAQUE WAS ERECTED IN 1991 BY GLOUCESTER CIVIC TRUST AND THE GLOUCESTERSHIRE SOCIETY FOR INDUSTRIAL ARCHAEOLOGY.

the tracks. Many such lines in Wales are now footpaths or bridleways, including one following the coastal path around Saundersfoot, several old tramways in Dyfed, and a number of paths in the Brecon Beacons south of Talybont-on-Usk. A similar situation has kept accessible a number of smaller tramways leading down from the Leigh and Tyldesley area of Lancashire to the Leeds & Liverpool Canal. Unfortunately, these paths now cross the fast dual-carriageway East Lancashire Road on the level, making them considerably less pleasant to explore.

It is important to note that even if 'disused tramway' is marked as such on a map, that it will not necessarily be a former horse-drawn line. Lines such as the Wantage Tramway in Oxfordshire, the Plynlimon & Hafan Tramway in West Wales and the various tramways serving quarries on the hills above Rossendale in Lancashire (though the latter two make very fine walks in themselves) were all entirely locomotive hauled on their level stretches.

Compared to former 'railways', engineering works are generally on a smaller scale. There are no really deep cuttings on our early lines, and few embankments either, though a fine one exists at Hawarden near Chester on the former Sandycroft Railway, and a slighter example took the Blaen-dare Tramroad through Pontypool. A couple of others feature in later chapters, as do a few of the best examples of tramroads being constructed on ledges.

Some very early viaducts well worth paying a visit include that at Langley Mill on the former Mansfield & Pinxton Railway, on the outskirts of the former town and the Kilmarnock & Troon Railway's bridge over the River Irvine at Fairlie. No longer visible due to infilling was the remarkable 1802 Blaenavon Viaduct, with a roof over the line and cottages between the arches. Also notable just east of Gathurst station on the still open Wigan to Southport route is a bridge constructed to carry the line over the originally wooden-tracked eighteenth-century Hustler's Railway, built to carry coal from pits near Orrell to the Leeds & Liverpool Canal.

So what are we still likely to find in place still in situ on the ground? Certainly nothing of any wooden structures – nor iron rails and nails, long since rusted away. But what you can see in many places – and which are the obvious trademarks of our routes – are the original stone sleeper blocks – sometimes stretching for quite some distance. On closer inspection you may well be able to see two or more holes in the top of each block where the nails went to secure the rails.

Bridge at Gathurst near Wigan. The former Lancashire & Yorkshire Railway's Wigan to Southport line is carried by a bridge over the eighteenth-century Hustler's Railway. The adjoining road bridge gives an idea of its diminutive size. (Author)

Stone sleeper blocks at the site of pointwork, Buxworth Basin, Peak Forest Tramway and Canal, Derbyshire. (Author)

Let us turn now to established footpaths (and cycle tracks) on former tramroads. Fortunately we have a ready made guide: *Vinter's Railway Gazetteer* – published in 2011 by The History Press. This invaluable work lists all former railways that can be walked officially over 2 miles in length on a county by county basis, and for the tramroad explorer is particularly useful in Wales where a number of conversions have taken place. Do remember though that there are several shorter paths along former tramroads that don't feature in the following chapter.

Let us now imagine we are looking for just such a line with the most minimal remains. We have identified the route from an old map, and do not believe that much has been built over. One possible way of finding out more without leaving home is by using the 'Google Earth' facility, or aerial photographs to get a view from above which should indicate (or not) the continued existence of the old formation. Even where nothing remains above ground, stones may exist below and sometimes after a period of dry weather this can lead to the tell-tale sign of grass being less green or crops growing less than on the soil above the stones.

But our next problem is going to be access – is the land owned privately, and if so can you find out by whom? Trespass is a civil (not criminal) offence in England and Wales, though damage to property, which includes crops, might very well be criminal. So it is a much better idea to identify the landowners and write or phone for permission to enter their land. Having given a good reason, many (but not all) landowners will be fine, and some of these will be prepared to assist you with names and contact details for the next landowners up or down the line. But if a landowner says no their decision has to be respected and they don't have to give any reason or justification for their decision.

You are most likely to get your first glimpse of the course of the tramroad where it crosses a road or public right of way. You may first want to know if road and tramway were there at the same time, if so there must have been some form of bridge or else a level crossing – but don't go looking for such things if the road was put through long after the tramway had closed. Similarly the presence of older houses or other buildings that would have contemporary to the tramroad can often give a clue to its course – but again you need to know the dates of operation of your tramroad and ideally have at least a little skill in aging houses and other buildings. In places tramways ran alongside existing roads and although this unfortunately often created an ideal opportunity for widening schemes alongside busy routes an unusually wide verge can be a tell-tale sign of a former line.

The selection of forty lines to walk and explore in the forthcoming chapter is by its very nature arbitrary – others might well have made different choices. I have deliberately chosen to include one or two very little-known tramroads as well as many of the best-known or most popular routes. Although a reasonably wide geographical spread has been achieved it must be admitted that the east and south-east of England are not as blessed with old tramroads as elsewhere, and those interested in such routes must, I am afraid, have to travel to more fruitful areas.

One in the South East worth remembering, though, is the Sittingbourne & Kemsley Light Railway; the preserved southern half of the former Bowater's Railway built to move the raw materials for paper making and also the finished products around the mill at Sittingbourne in Kent. Edward Lloyd, the newspaper owner and publisher, built Sittingbourne Mill in 1867 to supply his empire with paper. The railway was originally horse drawn and was centred around the wharf on Milton Creek with lines into storage sheds and the mill. It was only in 1905 that the first steam traction arrived in the form of 2 Kerr Stuart 'Brazil' class locomotives.

Tramways and Waggonways by Region

DEVON AND CORNWALL

The Cornish Mineral Tramways: Portreath to Devoran

Our most south-westerly walk is also one of our best and deservedly popular. It is in fact two separate tramroads, the Portreath Tramway and the Redruth & Chasewater Railway, joined together and linking the north and south coasts of Cornwall. Starting from Portreath Harbour north of Redruth on the B3300 on the north coast of Cornwall, the line commenced operation in 1809, largely to transport copper, with a 6-mile route to Crofthandy in operation by 1819. By the 1840s Portreath Harbour was busy with boats carrying copper ore to South Wales and bringing supplies of coal back with them. After the 1860s the demand for copper reduced, but the mining industry still had periods of prosperity, allowing the tramway to continue operation until closure at the end of 1935.

At somewhere between 11 and 15 miles (allowing for some worthwhile diversions) walking, the line forms a full day out, although it will be necessary to do some careful planning of bus journeys beforehand if leaving the car behind.

Beginning at Portreath Harbour (GR 657454) which, surrounded by rocks and cliffs, is spectacular in itself and around the outer harbour can be seen the sites of cranes which once exchanged goods between boats and waggons. Leaving the harbour, a short section of trackbed has been obliterated but causes few problems as the line can be quickly picked up on Sunnyvale Road as it heads east towards Scorrier. Distinctly tramway in character, stone sleeper blocks abound; some in obvious rows, others less easy to pick out.

Entering the Poldice Valley, the remains of arsenic works are passed, a stark reminder of the dangers faced by miners. A little further on you

Trackbed of Portreath Tramroad with sleeper blocks in situ. (Author)

reach the Redruth & Chasewater Railway for the run to the south coast. Whilst the Portreath line remained horsedrawn to the end, its southern neighbour was an early convert to locomotive power, using its first engine in 1854. Continuing through the valley, the village of Twelveheads is reached, exporter of miners to far flung places such as Lancashire (a gravestone in Bacup Cemetery commemorates a nineteenth-century Twelveheads-born quarry worker) and South America. The latter part of the line, again a well-surfaced footpath, follows the River Carnon towards Devoran where a wharf was situated. The main feature of this section is the crossing, of the still-open Truro to Falmouth branch line railway on a high, stone-arched viaduct. Adjacent are the stone pillars that supported Brunel's original wooden-trestled structure, replaced early in the twentieth century. At Devoran (GR 807390) the village hall was formerly a railway workshop.

Treffry's Railway: Luxulyan to Ponts Mill

Joseph Thomas Treffry was a mining entrepreneur who first made his name building a harbour at Par and a canal from the Luxulyan Valley down to Par. By the late 1830s, Treffry was turning to tramroads, the line from Pontsmill to Bugle, construction of which started around 1841 and was completed in 1847. Like all Treffry's subsequent lines, this one was built to standard gauge despite being designed for horse haulage. It commenced with a steep initial cable-hauled incline, and then followed the eastern edge of the Luxulyan Valley before crossing the impressive Treffry Viaduct to Luxulyan and Bugle. A branch just before the Treffry Viaduct to Colcerrow served several granite quarries in the area, which provided the stone for the construction of the viaduct. In 1855 the Pontsmill to Bugle line was extended to Par Harbour alongside the Par Canal, thus removing the need to tranship goods at Pontsmill.

In addition Treffry built an extension from what became the GWR station at Newquay down a 1 in 4 gradient to the harbour. This was always horse drawn and operated from the station's opening in 1849 until 1926. This also forms a pleasant, if short, footpath. It was always Treffry's intent to create a connection between the two lines and thus link Newquay on Cornwall's northern coast, with Par on the south. However, this was not achieved in his lifetime, nor by the Treffry Tramways in their original form. They were eventually rebuilt for locomotive haulage and a line was built to link between the two networks, so even today stretches of the tramway route are still in use by the line between Par and Newquay.

Treffry Viaduct, Treffry Railway. (Bertram Baxter collection)

Now a World Heritage Site, a 2-mile stretch of walkable tramroad can be picked up from the south end of Luxulyan station (GR 047582). Stone sleepers may be seen at intervals, as can a couple of short pieces of original rail. The main delight of this walk, however, is to be able to walk across Treffry's original 1847 viaduct. This also carries a water supply, which helped ensure that it received some maintenance before its historical value was recognised. The viaduct may be found at GR 056572, and consists of ten arches, each spanning 40ft and a maximum height of around 89ft. Should you see a multiple unit ambling along the Newquay branch below, it looks very small indeed.

The tramway path ends at Points Mill, GR 073562 from where onward travel or a return journey back down the tramroad may be made.

Decking of Treffry Viaduct. (Chris McFarlane)

The Plymouth & Dartmoor Railway

In the early nineteenth century granite was much in demand for buildings, bridges and other such structures and the owner of lands on Dartmoor gained royal assent in 1819 for a tramroad to run between Crabtree Wharf on the Laira Estuary at Plymouth and Kings Tor near Princetown. The Plymouth & Dartmoor Railway, opened in 1823, was a 4ft 6in gauge line using chaired rails bolted to granite setts. Granite and peat was the main traffic but general merchandise, much of it to Dartmoor Prison, was conveyed in the opposite direction.

A horse and waggon on the Plymouth & Dartmoor Railway, 1931. (Bertram Baxter collection)

A branch to Cann Quarry was opened in 1829; it was busy until 1855 and worked spasmodically until 1900. The South Devon Railway purchased the Sutton Harbour branch in 1851, converted it to mixed 4ft 6in/7ft gauge in 1857 and finally removed the 4ft 6in line when loco haulage was introduced in 1869.

From the line's southern terminus at Sutton Harbour (GR 485541) it headed east for half a mile alongside the later GWR branch then turned north-east alongside the estuary of the River Plym. It then headed north and after passing through Leigham tunnel traced a twisting path as it

followed the contours high above the west side of the Plym Valley to Yelverton. A branch to Cann Quarry left the 'main line' at Crabtree and soon bridged the River Plym at Marsh Mills. It then followed the east bank of the river, after crossing the Roborough to Plympton road on the level it passed under the GWR line to continue north for a mile until it finally passed beneath the GWR's Cann Viaduct into the quarry workings (GR 523596).

Short lengths of rails around Sutton Harbour survive but no walkable stretches remain here. The 2½ miles between Leigham Tunnel and Rumfle Quarry, however, is now a public footpath through the National Trust

Tree-lined trackbed on the Plymouth & Dartmoor Railway. (Bertram Baxter collection)

Plymbridge Woods. A frequent bus service exists or cars can also be parked at the end of this road where a stile gives access to Plymbridge Woods and the tramway. The route can be followed beyond Rumfle Quarry as far as GR 520601 but a detour is necessary though an Industrial Estate. The route can then be followed for a further 3 miles as it contours around a side valley of the Plym to Backeven Hill (GR 510624). The whole of the Cann Quarry route along the east bank of the River Plym can also be walked, including many stone setts and a two-span iron bridge over the Plym at Marsh Mills (now designated an ancient monument) together with an adjacent weighbridge cottage. Higher Leigham Tunnel, 620 yards long and 9ft 6in high, cut through solid rock is also visible, though with both portals generally sealed. During the Second World War it was used as an air-raid shelter. Granite tramway setts, placed at 6ft intervals, are visible throughout, especially in Plymbridge Woods but rails are now scarce; though several of the original cylindrical granite milestones can still be seen.

In walking the Yelverton to Princetown route the would-be explorer needs to understand the extent of the 1883 conversion to locomotive haulage; the railway company aimed to reuse as much of the formation as possible but did have to straighten out some very tight curves. This meant a longer route around Burrator. The new line also did not serve the original railhead at Foggintor Quarry (GR 588735, incidentally the source of stone for Nelson's Column). The quarry itself is well worth a visit, with drilled granite sleepers strewn around amongst loading platforms and half-collapsed buildings. In a National Park setting of unspoilt moorland both earlier and later formations are easily followed.

The Haytor Granite Tramway

This tramway was built to transport granite from quarries near Haytor Rock some 10 miles horizontally and 1,300ft vertically to the basin of the Stover Canal and opened in 1820 without need of an Act of Parliament. The unique feature of the Haytor line was that the rails or tramplates were hewn from irregular blocks of solid granite laid directly on the ground. The gauge of the track was 4ft 3in and at turnouts (points) the wheels were guided by wooden 'point tongues' of oak, pivoted on the granite-block rails. In the upward direction, the empty trams were pulled to the quarries by teams of horses; the loaded trams were run downhill by gravity to the Stover Canal basin at Ventiford near Teigngrace. The Stover Canal had been built by James Templer in 1770 for the clay traffic and was extended to Teigngrace in 1820; the tramway opening, with due ceremony, on 20 September of that year. Due to early financial mismanagement both

Track on the Haytor Granite Tramway. (Bertram Baxter collection)

the canal and the tramway were sold to Edward Adolphus Seymour, the eleventh Duke of Somerset, in 1829. The tramway's last use was sometime in the 1870s after which the encroachment of heather and other vegetation made parts of it impassable.

The gradients were laid out so that no single part of the line required more horses to be added as 'assisting engines'. A siding at Manaton Road may have been used to allow trains to pass. The wooden flat-topped waggons had iron flangeless wheels and ran in trains of usually twelve waggons drawn by eighteen horses in single file, quite a sight, in front for the upward journey and at the rear for the downward. The vehicles were thought to have been adapted road waggons.

Accidents were not uncommon as the only braking was provided by the horses and long wooden poles forced against the wheels. The granite rails had L-shaped grooves with the flanges on the inside and ran a parallel course, whilst some of the points were large blocks of solid granite. The rail granite setts (stone sleepers) were between 4–8ft long, curves being achieved by laying a series of short 'rails' on the inside of the curves. The iron wheels soon wore the straight granite flanges into shape on the curves.

Owing to the nature of the 'rails' large parts of the old tramway still exist, especially in the area below Haytor itself. Of particular interest are the complex points from which trucks were directed down different lines of the tramway, originally with a movable 'iron shoe' portion to direct the trains. Parts of the old track are now to be found in hedges, walls, bridges and gardens. Perhaps the best walkable section is that from Ullacombe (GR 782777), via Haytor Vale to Holwell Tor (GR 750778) which includes 2 miles of in situ track and some good examples of pointwork.

The Rattlebrook Peat Railway

The peaty head basin of the Rattlebrook attracted a few adventurers willing to try to extract and process the peat for naptha fuel. They all failed – but considerable sums were spent in constructing a railway up to the desolate and remote works at Rattlebrook some 350m higher up the moor. This standard gauge railway which started at exchange sidings just to the north-east of Bridestowe station is one of Dartmoor's least known railways.

   The line, constructed in 1879 for the Duchy of Cornwall, was 7 miles long and in that distance rose 1,000ft. It was operated for almost all of

Curved cutting on the Rattlebrook Peat Railway. (Author)

its life by horse and had only one passing place, just over halfway along the line from Bridestowe where the line reversed direction. At Rattlebrook there was an assortment of buildings and kilns for drying the peat which was brought from the cuttings by trucks run on a network of narrow gauge lines. At one time the operation employed around 100 men. Only in the final days of the railway was there any form of mechanisation, when a petrol lorry was converted at Oakhampton to run on rails. Its final job in 1932 was to remove all the metal as scrap from Rattlebrook and lift the rails, after which the peat works were served by lorries which forced their way up and down the formation.

Access, at least by car, is quite straightforward, though buses in the area are somewhat scarce. It is best to head for the small car park (GR 526853) just up the track from the Dartmoor Inn on the Okehampton to Tavistock road from where access can readily be gained. The whole of the line can be followed on foot, though having had a rough road laid on the formation after closure it is a rather more stony and uneven surface than other such lines. After curving back on itself after it leaves the exchange sidings at Bridestowe, the route forms an irregular inverted 'V' shape, including a point of reversal. By using footpaths across the top of the moors it is possible to devise a triangular route which will bring the explorer back to the start point. The railway track is certainly a splendid way of getting to see this part of Dartmoor.

The lines described above by no means exhaust all the possibilities here. In Cornwall others worthy of exploration include the Pentewan Railway near St Austell and the Liskeard & Caradon Railway at Moorswater. In Devon further exploration is possible on the Redlake Railway and the Zeal Tor Tramroad (uniquely built with wooden rails attached to granite setts) as well as a number of more minor lines.

DORSET & SOMERSET

The Portland Railway (The Merchants' Railway)

Portland is a remarkable place, maintaining its beauty despite hundreds of years of quarrying which has quite literally carved away large parts of the island, some of it being used for buildings as famous as St Paul's Cathedral. From the Portland Heights the views are famous, covering the full 360 degrees with the surrounding sea looking as blue as anywhere on our coastline. Castletown is where the building stone was shipped from the island and where you will find the Merchants' Railway, West Dorset's first ever railway system. The line on Portland opened in 1826 and ran until

A scene of desolation on the Portland Railway after closure. (Bertram Baxter collection)

the start of the Second World War in 1939; it was largely lifted in 1957. Only one type of waggon was required to carry the stone, this consisted of four-wheeled trolleys with dumb buffers and no springs. The method of operation had not appreciably changed during the 133 years of operation, and the Merchant's Railway was considered by some to be the outstanding example of a horse worked railway in the west of England. The railway, with its 4ft 6in gauge, was never physically connected to other lines; however, after the opening of Weymouth & Portland Railway in 1865, an exchange siding was constructed, so that the stone could be transferred either to ship or to standard gauge railway waggons.

Our route starts next to the old castle (GR 685743), close to the above mentioned exchange sidings and at the foot of what is known as

Incline on the Portland Railway. (Author)

Freeman's Incline or the Merchants Incline. Soon the stone sleeper blocks clearly identify the track as a tramway – all the while you are climbing straight up the hill. Once up the incline and through an old bridge with a modern inner lining, you have a choice of routes.

The right-hand track will take you on a slightly lower path, surprisingly close to the backs of modern houses, then up a second incline. This incline has three bridges and a stony base, slippery after rain, with grooves where the rails once lay still clear in the foundation. The left-hand track, initially at a slightly higher level, curves the opposite way round and reaches the same quarries, the two tracks thus allowing an unusual form of two-way working. Once up the level of the quarries, the choice of routes is yours, as there is an array of routes along the tops and sides of the various quarries. One landmark here is the strangely named Nicodemus' Knob, a limestone stack left behind by quarrymen whose height gives a vivid idea of how much of Portland has been quarried away.

The Tramways of Purbeck (Middlebere Plateway and Fayle's Tramway)

Purbeck's tramroads make for a fascinating day out and are set in a location where much has been preserved. One can even combine the day's tramway exploration with a ride behind a steam locomotive, as the Swanage Railway's 'park and ride' station at Nodern is right in the heart of tramroad country.

Our first tramway was Dorset's first, the Middlebere Plateway, which was built across Hartland Moor very early in the nineteenth century by a wealthy London merchant – Benjamin Fayle – to take ball clay from his pits near Corfe Castle to boats moored on Poole Harbour. The engineer responsible for its construction was John Hodgkinson, whose mentor

Horses and waggons on the Middlebere Plateway, 1890. (Author's collection)

and cousin was Benjamin Outram. Contemporary accounts indicate that the line was built in 1805 and opened in 1806, and it is clearly shown on a local map of 1811. Initially the railway served clay pits to the east side of the road from Wareham to Corfe Castle, but shortly thereafter it was extended by means of a tunnel to serve clay workings on the other side of the road. There are two tunnels under the road, serving different workings. The northern tunnel carries a plaque on its east face reading 'BF 1807'. The southern tunnel has a plaque on its west face dated 1848, but as the tunnel is shown on earlier maps this is believed to be a rebuilding date.

Two horses worked in tandem pulling five waggons weighing almost a ton each and with a 2-ton capacity. They made three round trips a day, giving an annual total of 9,000–10,000 tons. By 1865 an additional team of horses and waggons had been brought into use and additional passing places were constructed, which enabled the annual tonnage to

Fayle's First Tunnel on the Middlebere Plateway, Purbeck. The inscription on the headstone is for Benjamin Foyle: BF 1807. (Author)

be raised to 22,000 tons. However, by the late 1800s the plateway's days were numbered. The channel at Middlebere was silting up, limiting the size of vessel that could approach the quay. The Middlebere Plateway was eventually abandoned in about 1907, when it was replaced by Fayle's Tramway, which connected Fayle's clay works at Norden with their works at Newton and thence to Poole Harbour at Goathorn. Fayle's Tramway took over much of the plateway's trackbed in the Norden area, including the exchange siding and the bridge over the main line railway. However, the plateway's main route to Middlebere Creek, and the tunnels under the railway and road were all abandoned.

As a plateway, the Middlebere Plateway differed from the edge railway that eventually became the norm, in that the flanges retaining the truck wheels on the line were on the rails (plates) rather than on the wheels. The plates were 3ft long, L-shaped and made of cast iron, weighing around 40lb. They were supported on stone sleepers weighing about 60–70lb each; the ends of the plates were held down by nails driven into wooden plugs inserted into holes in the sleepers. The gauge was thought to have been 3ft 9in, although recent archaeological investigations suggest it may have been a little narrower, perhaps 3ft 6in.

A few remains of the Middlebere Plateway are still visible. The quay at Middlebere Creek has gradually fallen into disrepair and almost vanished. Some of the stone sleepers remain in place today, complete with holes where the rails used to be fixed, whilst others have been reused as paving stones at various locations. In many places the route across Hartland Moor can be traced. The iron bridge over the main line railway, first built for the plateway and then used by Fayle's Tramway, still stands. A 2-mile section of the Middlebere Plateway, from Norden Heath (GR 951835) to Middlebere Farm (GR 963853), from where it has been reused as an access road to the farm, is an officially designated footpath.

The later Fayle's Tramway also has a 2-mile section of official path, from Bushey (GR981835) to Newton Heath (GR 001884), but much of this and the shorter Pike Bros Tramway is on freely accessible land. Benjamin Fayle's old plateway is particularly useful here, not least because it provides a firm surface over what can otherwise be damp ground. The railway's route can be followed south towards Corfe for more than a mile but it should be noted that the Middlebere Quay is not accessible by members of the public. The location is in full view of a pair of bird hides and forms part of an important bird sanctuary. However, the National Trust occasionally allow supervised access by means of guided walks to the site.

The Somerset Coal Canal Tramway: Radstock to Wellow

First a canal (though never used as such), then a tramway and finally a main line railway – it is hardly surprising that following the old route from Midford to Wellow and on to Radstock can be somewhat confusing at times.

Let us start with the Somerset Coal Canal, leaving the Kennet & Avon Canal at Limpley Stoke then, shortly after passing under the A36 road, the Radstock Canal branch veered south-west.

When the Radstock branch was constructed, it was intended to link it to the main line of the Paulton Branch at Midford, which was at a lower level at this point. The Lock Fund created in 1802 was to have paid for the construction of the locks, but because there was little regular traffic on the branch, the company built one lock, an aqueduct over the Midford Brook, and a short tramway to bridge the gap. This contributed to the economic failure of the branch, and its replacement by a tramway in 1815. The tramway was laid along the former canal's towpath. It was single-line with passing places every 600 yards and was originally laid using cast-iron plates on stone block sleepers, but was relaid using wrought-iron plates. The story goes that if two drivers met between passing places they would resort to fisticuffs with the winner gaining precedence. The tramway finally closed in 1874 when the Somerset & Dorset's Railway extension to Bath was largely built along its route from Radstock to Midford.

So what we will see are largely the remains of the Somerset & Dorset Railway, closed after much controversy in January 1966. Starting at Waterloo Road, just off Radstock's town centre (GR694550), a 2-mile stretch follows the trackbed, followed by a further section of about a mile largely along a footpath just to the north of the former line as far as Shoscombe Vale (GR 727564). The Paulton Branch ran parallel to what became the Great Western Railway's route between Radstock and Midsomer Norton, with the 'five arches' bridge which carried the Somerset & Dorset Railway built across it, rather than over it.

At Wellow, the Somerset & Dorset took a more direct line through the village, and as such, a short piece of original tramway on a curve still remains. This incorporates a short tunnel near the village church, but it must be stressed that this lies on private land and should not be accessed without permission. From Wellow to Midford one can return to the trackbed, but here the route is permissive rather than officially public and do note that dogs are not permitted on this stretch. There is much to see at Midford (GR 761607) including the impressive S&D viaduct and station, the formation of the former GWR Camerton to Limpley Stoke route and the Midford Canal basin.

Wellow Tunnel near Radstock on the Somerset Coal Canal's Tramway. It was originally built for a canal branch. (Phillip Earnshaw)

The Dramway (Avon & Gloucestershire Railway)

This line forms our first example of a more 'urban' route, just a few miles east of the city of Bristol, and as such the survival of so much of it can be considered remarkable.

In the 1820s a proposal was put forward for a horse-drawn railway to be built from Ram Hill Pit in Coalpit Heath to wharfs on the Avon at Keynsham. Construction work began in 1829 and in November 1830 the Dramway transported its first waggon loads of coal.

After the opening of the line between Shortwood and Bristol on the 6 August 1835, the Bristol & Gloucestershire Railway had its mind on expansion and planned a broad gauge link northwards towards Gloucester. The northern section of the Dramway between Shortwood and the junction with Ram Hill Pit was converted during 1844, and in the process became the first mixed gauge track in the country. However, problems arose with mixed horse and locomotive-drawn traffic and eventually the B&GR decided that the cost of such modifications would be more than the traffic was worth; the coal that flowed from the pits at Coalpit Heath, before the suspension of traffic on 5 June 1844 for the building of the broad gauge line, proved to be the last from those pits to traverse the Dramway.

From Shortwood to the River Avon at Keynsham, the route descends 176ft in height over a length of just over 5¼ miles. The track consisted of cast-iron fish-bellied rail that sat in chairs attached to stone sleeper blocks. The horses walked between the rails on a coal ash path and a man walked alongside the waggons, ready to apply the brakes. On the descent the horses

Trackbed of the Dramway north of Bitton, near Bristol. (Author)

would have had little to do, but on the ascent they would have worked hard, especially on the 1 in 76 section of line north of Willsbridge Road. Each of the waggons on the Dramway held 4 tons of coal – twice the capacity of those on similar such lines.

By the 1860s the Great Western Railway who had earlier gained ownership of the tramway had decided the Dramway was no longer needed and obtained the necessary powers under the GWR (Additional Powers) Act to abandon the route. The final waggon load of coal was sent from Hole Lane Pit in January 1867. Part of the line, though, was to get a surprise reprieve in 1881 when the owner of California Colliery at Willsbridge reopened the southern section to get his coal down to the Avon at Keynsham.

The end came in March 1904 when a tremendous flood burst through the workings of California Colliery and miners barely escaped with their lives. This catastrophe bankrupted the Oldland Colliery Company and the pit closed. On 9 July 1906 the GWR Traffic Committee was informed that all traffic along the route had ceased and that the Dramway had officially closed, never to reopen. In 1935 the GWR sold the section of the A&GR between California Colliery and Willsbridge to the Bristol Water Works. They used it to lay a water main from the pit to Willsbridge. During the Second World War, Willsbridge Tunnel was used as an air-raid shelter.

Today the majority of the line has been converted to a well-signposted footpath from Coalpit Heath (GR 675806), though part of the route north of Mangotsfield disappeared under a recently constructed bypass. It is also

Inside Willsbridge Tunnel, 'Dramway'. (Author)

possible to view (though not enter) Willsbridge and Westoncourt Tunnels at the southern end of the route close to the River Avon where the line terminated (GR 662699). The line's terminus at Ram Hill has recently been restored and is particularly worth viewing.

SOUTH WALES

The Saundersfoot Railway

The 4ft gauge Saundersfoot Railway was built in 1829, primarily to carry coal from the developing Daucleddau coalfield where Saundersfoot was rapidly developing as an industrial centre; by 1846 seven collieries were using the line. It was the first railway in Pembrokeshire and remained

independent until the end. The company's original Act forbade locomotives but did authorise passenger traffic though these were never carried. It consisted of two main mineral lines and a number of small branches and was originally worked tramway style by pairs of horses pulling three loaded drams. One main line connected Stepaside/Kilgetty Collieries & Ironworks (a mile east of Kilgetty railway station) to Saundersfoot Harbour, running along the coast through a series of short tunnels. In Saundersfoot itself, what is now The Strand was originally known as Railway Street where it passed through the town. The other line ran from Saundersfoot Harbour to Reynalton. It went up an incline of 1 in 5 approximately half a mile from the harbour, passed beneath the GWR station in a narrow long tunnel (GR 124060) of around 400 yards in length and continued in a north-westerly direction to Broom and Thomas Chapel Collieries and in 1914 an extension to Reynalton Quarry took the line 1–2 miles beyond Reynalton. This closed in 1921.

The line's success was based on the continuing success of the collieries in the area and as such by 1874 it became necessary to relay the whole line with

Incline on the Saundersfoot Railway. Note the use of three rails except at the halfway point where waggons crossed. (Bertram Baxter collection)

The shortest of the three tunnels on the Saundersfoot Railway. (Author)

flat-bottom rails on wooden sleepers, enabling the use of locomotives from that date onwards. By the late 1920s the industry was in recession and the line at a standstill, though in 1932 a brief renaissance in the local mines lead to the line becoming active again, however, adverse economic and geological conditions prevailed and by 1939 the mines were silent for good.

A section of the route follows the coast from Saundersfoot (GR 137048) to Stepaside (GR 138077) and is very attractive as it weaves along the coastline passing through three tiny (in dimension) tunnels (illuminated where required) built into the cliffs.

The Swansea & Mumbles Railway

In March 1807, a converted railway waggon was drawn by horses from Swansea to Mumbles. The people on board the waggon made a historic journey: they were the first ever railway passengers.

The railway had originally been constructed to serve mining and quarrying operations at Mumbles, facilitating the transport of minerals to Swansea Dock. Until then, they had been transported by boat across Swansea Bay. An initial meeting was held at the Bush Inn, Swansea, in July 1804, and by the spring of 1806 goods were being transported by rail along the coast to Swansea Docks. These were carried in horse-drawn waggons;

Postcard of horse and 'carriage' on the Swansea & Mumbles Railway. (Bertram Baxter collection)

The former station building at Oystermouth on the Swansea & Mumbles Railway. (Steve Gilligan)

the early experiments with steam locomotives had yet to yield any great successes. As described earlier, Richard Trevithick had been working on such a project at Merthyr Tydfil and, though initial tests were successful, his 7-ton locomotive proved too heavy for the rails in use at the time.

One of the men involved in laying the Swansea–Mumbles line was Benjamin French. He had the idea of transporting passengers along the line, and paid the line owners the sum of £20 per year to provide this service. Begun in March 1807, it proved popular among wealthy tourists, and the service flourished. By the 1860s steam power was introduced, and by 1898 the line had been extended to the lighthouse at Mumbles,

and a pier was constructed to attract more passengers. By the 1920s the train carried up to 1,800 passengers per journey, crammed into double-decker carriages. Its considerable weight allowed speeds of only 5mph, and the journey could take up to an hour. The line was electrified in 1929, and trams replaced the steam locomotive.

In 1958, only four years after an extravagant 150th anniversary celebration, it was announced that the railway was to close. It had been bought by a bus company, which planned to tear up the line and replace the service with their buses. The people of Swansea were outraged, and a barrister was hired by the 'Mumbles Pier Amusement Equipment Company' to fight the case in Parliament. However, the barrister withdrew within twelve hours of the hearing, and there was insufficient time to properly brief a replacement. Parliament approved the proposal, and the oldest surviving railway in the UK and the first ever to carry passengers, was dismantled in 1960.

Starting at the sparkling new National Waterfront Museum in Swansea it is an easy matter to follow the course of the tramway from GR 660924 to GR 630875 as it curves gently around the bay. For a while the formation is broader as the London & North Western Railway had a line that ran through Gowerton to points north and a fine footbridge crosses what is now a dual-carriageway road. After Black Pill the path becomes quieter and eventually, after passing Oystermouth station, now a tourist information office, the terminus at Mumbles pier is reached.

The Carmarthenshire Railway: Llanelli to Mynydd Mawr (Cross Hands)

The Llanelly & Mynydd Mawr Railway (LMMR) was established in 1802 in Carmarthenshire, Wales, as the Carmarthenshire Tramroad by Act of Parliament. It began running trains in 1803, the initial line being a

plateway of about 4ft gauge, with motive power provided by a pair of horses. This distribution line allowed for coal extraction in the hinterland to be connected to the Sandy area and Llanelli Docks and in 1798 the Stradey Iron Works established by Alexander Raby had begun trading and later received coal, ironstone and limestone for its furnaces via the Carmarthenshire line. The claim that the Llanelly & Mynydd Mawr Railway is the oldest public railway in Britain was supported by the following contemporary quotation: 'Construction continued apace and in May 1803 the line was open for traffic from the ironworks at Cymddyche down to the sea, a distance of one and a half miles'.

Skew Bridge on the Carmarthenshire Railway south of Cross Hands. (Author)

This short length of line can therefore lay claim to being the first public railway in use in Britain, because the better-known Surrey Iron Railway was not ready for traffic until July 1803. By that month it was reported that a further 3 miles of the Carmarthenshire Railway, together with certain branches, were already in use.

By 1844 the company ceased trading and it was to take nearly forty years for the line to re-emerge. Reopening took place in 1883, operated by the newly formed Llanelly & Mynydd Mawr Railway Company (LMMR). Throughout the twentieth century and into the nationalisation era the line continued as a main artery for coal distribution from the Gwendraeth Valley, until the closure of Cynheidre Colliery in 1989.

Now with an all-weather surface and forming part of National Cycle Network Route 47, the former Carmarthenshire line can be followed for as much as 12 miles from just west of Llanelli Docks (GR 499003) to Cross Hands (GR559132) through delightfully unspoilt countryside north of Llanelli. It needs saying, however, that the places the line served such as Cymheidre and Cross Hands still bear the scars of their former role as colliery villages, and as such cannot supply more than the most basic of facilities to the rambler or tramway explorer.

Hirwaun to Abernant and Penderyn Tramways

Hirwaun, north of Aberdare and close to the A465 heads of the valleys road, is the archetypal small south Welsh town, with an industrial background centring on its former ironworks. The ironworks was already in existence by the late eighteenth century and passed through a succession of owners before being purchased in 1819 by William Crawshay of Cyfarthfa, in whose family it remained until closure in 1859. The ironworks' blast furnaces required coke, which spurred an increase in local coal mining activities. Even after the ironworks closed, coal mining continued. Following the 1980s miners' strike, however, the only deep coal mine left in Wales was Tower Colliery, a couple of miles to the north of Hirwaun which had to close down, but was bought by its workers and reopened. It closed for a final time in early 2008.

Two tramways, either side of Hirwaun, may be explored and make fine walking on a clear day. Firstly Hirwaun to Penderyn, a horse-drawn

Trackbed with sleeper blocks on the Hirwaun to Abernant Tramway. (Bertram Baxter collection)

Buttressed cutting on Hirwaun to Abernant Tramway south of Hirwaun. (Author)

route which connected Penderyn's quarries with Hirwaun's blast furnaces. Opened in the mid-1780s, the line was converted to steam power in 1904, with diesels following. The line remained in use until 1982 and is now part of NCN46. The route has a gentle compacted stone surface, but it can get muddy in places after long spells of rain. There are also anti-motorcycle barriers at either end of the trail and at points along the trail. The Penderyn Quarry Line leaflet contains details on wildlife and historical features. The route runs parallel to the A4059 Hirwaun to Brecon road.

There are two start points: at Penderyn (GR 951085) cross the bridge just north of the Penderyn Whisky plant or at GR 959061 by crossing the railway line at the end of Penyard Road, Hirwaun.

The Hirwaun to Abernant Tramway (GR 965052 – 000032), last used in 1900, traverses somewhat less exposed countryside and is an official footpath and cycleway throughout. At one time many sleeper blocks remained, but these are less in evidence these days.

SOUTH-EAST WALES AND THE FOREST OF DEAN

The Brinore Tramroad

Without doubt one of Britain's classic tramway walks, the Brinore Tramroad was built in 1814–15 under a 1793 Act allowing construction of tramroads of up to 8 miles in length to link with the Brecknock & Abergavenny Canal. The clause allowed the B&A Company to construct tramroads to workings within this distance or owners of such workings to obtain wayleaves to do so. The 8-mile post, no longer to be found, would have been in Trefil, measured from the tramroad's canal wharf at Talybont.

Since the company declined to build it, the tramroad was built by public subscription at a cost of £12,800 and opened in 1815. An extension to serve the Rhymney Iron Works and the Bryn Oer collieries in the Rhymney Valley was built privately by Benjamin Hall, who was one of the chief sponsors of the Brinore Tramroad proper. The tramroad remained in use until around 1860–70, when it fell into disuse following a decline in traffic. The Brinore Tramroad Company was formed through an Act of Parliament but there is no evidence that it was formally dissolved. The legal ownership of the tramroad is therefore unclear, although public access, through its common carrier origins and bridleway status, is not in doubt.

The gauge of the tramroad was 3ft 6in and length of the tramplates was 47in. The tramroad was single-track, with just thirteen passing places spread throughout the 8 miles. The tramplates were spiked into the sleeper blocks only at the passing places: these sleeper blocks show the holes drilled to take the spikes.

Starting at Talybont-on-Usk (GR 116226) it is worth first visiting the tramroad's canal wharf, where there is an information board and replica tram opposite some fine limekilns, although the kilns themselves are on private land. A clear path up the Caerfanell Valley, gradually gaining height, with Talybont reservoir far below on your right, and the Brecon & Merthyr Railway far below and out of sight, can be followed to

Bridge at Pen Rhiw-Calch on the Brinore Tramroad. (Bertram Baxter collection)

Pen Rhiw-Calch, 'Head of the Limestone Valley'. This was the main interchange point along the line, where there were buildings, sidings, and at least one public house. The only bridge on the tramroad, here at Pen Rhiw-Calch, was largely demolished in 1958 and most traces were finally removed in 1997. A wooded section follows, with occasional spectacular views of a meadow and farmhouse surrounded by hills on three sides. The tramroad continues south towards Ffos y Wern, reaching the head of the Sirhowy Valley. North of Trefil the line follows the course of a rough road leading to a quarry, eventually branching off to traverse the side of the Dyffryn Crawnon Valley in a spectacular horseshoe-curved path. This last section is badly affected by landslips and some care is required to climb over mounds of earth and fallen blocks of limestone. Eventually the line

Horseshoe curve on the Brinore Tramroad. (Bertram Baxter collection)

reaches a minor road on the site of the formation, leading to the end of
the tramroad at Trevil (GR 108152).

The Penydarren Tramway

The Merthyr Tramway, better known as the Penydarren Tramway, was
opened in 1802, built by the Dowlais, Penydarren and Plymouth Ironworks
as a joint project. It ran from Merthyr to the canal basin at Abercynon,
a distance of 9½ miles The gauge was 4ft 2in inside the plate flanges,
or 4ft 4in over them and was single track with frequent passing loops.

Plymouth Tunnel on the Penydarren Tramway. (Phillip Earnshaw)

The tramroad clung to the hillside on the east side of the Taff for almost all the way, with a gentle average gradient, suitable for horses, of 1 in 145. It had three engineering features of note. At Plymouth works, the line passed right underneath the charging area of the furnaces in a tunnel, the first railway tunnel in Wales, 8ft high and 8ft wide: ample clearance for horse-drawn trams but a distinct impediment to locomotive working. Further south, two bridges carried the line across a large loop of the Taff near Quakers Yard, both of which began life as timber structures. However, on 16 February 1815 it was reported that: 'The upper Tram Road Bridge near Quakers Yard fell down yesterday while the Penydarren Trams were going over it. The whole of the Iron, Trams, Horses & Hallier fell into the river as well as 4 other Persons who were riding on the Trams'. In the event, both bridges were quickly replaced by large elliptical stone arches, each spanning 63ft, with the deck about 32ft above the water. Both survive as outstanding examples of early railway bridges and are now scheduled ancient monuments.

Victoria Bridge; the lower of the two bridges on the Penydarren Tramway. (Author's collection)

By 1851 the Dowlais ironworks had stopped using the Penydarren Tramway and the stretch from Dowlais to the Penydarren works was presumably abandoned at the same time. Thereafter the tramroad fell out of use piecemeal. When Penydarren works closed in 1859 the section down to Plymouth was probably closed too. Plymouth went on sending some iron down to Abercynon for a while, but ceased to produce iron in 1880 and south of here the tramroad seems to have been lifted about 1890.

The line was immortalised by the running of the first ever steam train by Richard Trevithick's locomotive, when a load of 10 tons of iron and five waggons (plus various passengers) was hauled by a steam train on 21 February 1804. Amid great interest from the public it successfully ran the full distance down to Abercynon in four hours and five minutes, at an average speed of nearly 5mph. Witnesses included a Mr Giddy, a respected patron of Trevithick and an engineer from the government. However, some of the short cast-iron plates of the tramroad broke under the locomotive and so the tramroad returned to horse power after the initial test run. Trevithick's achievement is comemorated in a memorial outside the fire station in Abercynon.

The southern part of the route from Pontygwaith (GR 085949) to Abercynon is the most easily traced, though in February 2010, all that was missing was a cycle bridge over the A4060 on the southern edge of Merthyr before a continuous route was available right through to Abercynon (GR 081978). The two bridges over the Taff are to be found at GR 094962 and GR 090965.

Hill's Tramroad

The 2ft-gauge plateway railway built by Thomas Hill in the years after he began to manage Blaenavon Ironworks in 1812, known as Hill's Tramroad, provides clear evidence of technological developmental, as well as leaving us a legacy of one of Britain's most spectacular tramway paths. Hill's Tramroad was a 2ft gauge horse-drawn tramroad connecting the Tyla Quarry on Gilwern Hill with the Blaenavon Ironworks, and also providing a route past the Garnddyrys forge in Cwm Llanwenarth to the Brecon and Abergavenny Canal. Starting from a basin at Llanfoist (GR 285133), the railway was completed in 1817. By this means, the Blaenavon Company hoped to avoid the high tolls charged by the Monmouthshire Canal and to reach markets for their coal in the upper Usk Valley and to the east across the English border in Herefordshire. At Llanfoist there was a substantial warehouse for storing pig iron and wrought-iron bars and blooms before they were loaded on to canal boats. Pig iron from the Blaenavon Ironworks was taken to the forge at Garnddyrys to be forged into wrought iron, which then was taken along the railway to the canal.

The tramway is also notable for its tunnel at Pwll Du, opened around 1815–16; it is the longest on any horse-drawn line in Britain at just over 1¼ miles long. At the height of its active life the tunnel saw loads of some fifteen to twenty trams per day, each containing about 2 tons of limestone rock. Battery-operated bell wires were used in the tunnel to give stop, easing-off and go signals – respectively one, two or three taps. In winter time during the 1920s, John Powell, who operated the main stationary engine at the Blaenavon entrance, would take care to delay the trams should he see any Pwll Du women approaching in the distance. They used the tunnel as a short-cut in times of bad weather and rode through the hill seated on the trams. Eventually, with increasing production of coal and pig iron at Blaenavon, the Pwll Du tunnel could no longer cope with the volume of traffic. Thomas Dyne Steel was engaged in 1850 to design and construct a double incline railway crossing the mountain from near New Pit in Blaenavon to Pwll Du. A survey dating from 1933 showed a continuous route through without any evidence of collapse or obstruction, but the tunnel has long since been sealed off.

To follow the footpath along the course of the line, on a narrow ledge cut into the steep mountainsides, is a thrilling experience. Many of the original stone sleepers of the plateway are still visible. On rounding

Entrance to Pwll Du Tunnel, Hill's Tramway, the longest tramway tunnel in Britain. (Phillip Earnshaw)

the northern headland of the Blorenge look out for the 'Hilton Hotel' a 45-yard 'cut and cover' tunnel which dates from 1818 and is listed as an ancient monument. Continue along the track as it skirts to the left of the tunnel before rejoining the tramroad. Shortly afterwards, the end of the level tramroad is marked by retaining walls on your right. This area was originally a marshalling yard, where waggons were switched to the inclines on your left.

If you continue down the steep Llanfoist inclines you emerge at a wooden gate and stile at Llanfoist Wharf, on the Brecknock and Abergavenny Canal (completed in 1812). Here, having descended three sections of counterbalanced incline from the level tramroad 255m above, the products of the forge were transferred to barges for transport to Newport Docks.

Tramways around Brynmawr and Llangattock

These three tramroads in close proximity to each other make a superb day's walking.

During the mid-eighteenth century there arose in Abergavenny a desire to tap the wealth generated by the great ironworks of Merthyr and Dowlais together with the rapidly developing coal trade. The greater part of the length of the northern escarpment Mynydd Llangatwg or Llangattock Mountain is scarred by limestone quarries which operated for much of the nineteenth century. The rock was removed by means of a series of tramroads which headed north via steep inclines to a wharf on the Monmouthshire & Brecon Canal at Llangattock and south to Brynmawr and the ironworks at Nant-y-glo by two tramroads which contoured the eastern end of the hill. The upper tramway, which dates from the start of the nineteenth century, runs south from Pant-y-Gilwern and Daren Disgwylfa and then west around the head of Cwm Clydach. It is now a grassy footpath providing easy walking through otherwise rough terrain. The lower tramway was constructed in 1828–30 and has since been converted to a public road. Both tramroads had several branches to serve individual quarries along the escarpment. The hill is mapped as open access lane and therefore freely available for walkers to roam at will. There are many remnants of the coal, iron and lime industries on the remaining wharfs such as lime kilns at Llangattock and several tramways which carried coal, iron ore and limestone to and fro the industrial valleys to the west.

Starting at Llangattock (GR 204158), the Llangattock Tramroad can be followed as a public footpath to Darren Cilau Quarry (GR 205169). This line was used to convey limestone from Darren Cilau Quarry down to Llangattock Wharf on the Brecon & Merthyr Canal. The quarry is now a scheduled ancient monument. Just over a mile to the south-east of Darren Cilau Quarry is Darren Disgwylfa Quarry (GR 219142). From here you can follow the Darren Disgwylfa Tramroad for 2 miles to near Brynmawr (GR201124). This tramway was built by the Bailey family in 1811 to transport limestone down to Nantyglo Ironworks near Brynmawr.

From Brynmawr (GR 197121) a spectacular route can be followed to Llanfoist (GR 285133). This was originally the Clydach Rail Road, which opened in 1794, but was later sold to the Monmouth Railway & Canal Company for conversion to a conventional railway in 1864, later becoming what was known as the LNWR's Heads of the Valleys line. This route, running through the Clydach Gorge, now forms one of the best railway paths in Wales, if not the whole of the UK. Even by nineteenth-century standards, the construction costs must have been astronomical. The surface is tarmac except for the section just down from the upper tunnels (where it remains grassy ballast) and, for the most part, the line followed is the later railway rather than the original tramway. The tunnels are bypassed using the line of the tramway, some of which has been taken over by shared access to houses and a short stretch of public highway; the tramway gets around the upper tunnels by climbing dramatically high up a wooded cliff. One of the upper tunnels can be walked through but it is unsurfaced, unlit and pitch black in the middle due to the curve; if you intend to walk this, it is essential to bring a torch. Both lower tunnels are blocked.

The Forest of Dean Railways

The Forest of Dean in west Gloucestershire was a centre of industry for centuries, based not only on timber but also on stone, iron ore, charcoal and later coal. By 1787 coal production in the Forest had risen to 90,000 tons, with thirty-seven pits at Parkend alone. The Forest roads at this time were impassable in winter and unsuited to the heavy traffic and so a system of tramroads, completed by 1812, was built by three companies. Two of them, the Severn & Wye Company, and the Forest of Dean Company, ran to purpose-built ports on the Severn at Lydney and Bullo Pill. The tramroads used L-section flanged plates, with a gauge of around 3ft 6in, over which waggons with flangeless wheels were pulled by horses, ponies or mules. The network was very extensive, with branches and spurs servicing the pits, quarries and stoneworks in the area. Given that so many of the disused railways in this area were conversions from former tramroads, there is much to explore and it is only possible here to point out a few sites of particular interest.

An evocative pre-war photograph of traffic on the Severn & Wye Railway, Forest of Dean. (Bertram Baxter collection)

Tramway Tunnel on the Milkwall Branch near Coleford, Forest of Dean. (Author)

Commercial narrow gauge tramroads reached the Wye Valley very early. In 1811, the Severn & Wye Tramroad linked Lydney to Lydbrook, allowing coal and iron ore to be easily moved. This greatly helped industrial development at Lydbrook, where a wharf beside the river became a major centre for transport throughout the UK and overseas. The route of this tramroad can still be followed to the east of Lower Lydbrook at Bishopswood. In later years, some of the main lines became steam-hauled railways, including the Forest of Dean Railway Company's line, which was converted to a broad gauge line by the South Wales Railway in 1854, but many of the tramway branches continued to work with horses. Some were remarkably long lived, the Wimbery Slade tramway lasting until the 1930s and Bixslade to 1947.

As industry in the Forest went into a slow decline, the Severn–Wye line eventually became the last remaining railway into the Forest and was closed by British Rail in 1976. The line was purchased for preservation by Dean Forest Railway in 1985 and slowly upgraded to Lydney Junction, by 1995, to provide a connection with the national network.

THE MIDLANDS

The Brill Tramway

This line started out as a horse-drawn tramway to serve the estate of the 3rd Duke of Buckingham and Chandos and was originally known as the Wotton Tramway. Two horses were used to draw up to three goods 'carriages' along most of the line, though they could only manage to pull a single carriage when the gradient got too steep on a heavy load.

Building started in 1870, with Brill station being the last to be completed in April 1872. Initially, the single-track line was constructed for the transportation of goods and minerals for local farms and works, and only estate workmen and people accompanying live stock were permitted to travel on the line but locals demanded a passenger service and a suitable carriage was borrowed. With the advent of the passenger service, it was realised that the original horse locomotion wasn't enough so an Aveling & Porter steam locomotive was bought, an engine specifically designed for use on a tramway such as this.

An attempt was made in 1873 to upgrade the tramway's status to that of being legally recognised as a railway, but this failed as the tramway didn't meet many of the criteria required. Specifically, at this point in time there was no signalling, and no accommodation for level-crossing operators (these were operated by the train driver himself). With Quainton Road increasingly seeing more traffic, the duke saw the potential of extending his tramway west to Oxford and an Act of Parliament was granted in 1888 to allow the extension, though it was never built.

Today a good stretch of over 2 miles can be followed from Quainton Road station (GR 737189, now the Buckingham Railway Centre), clearly signposted as the Brill Tramway Walk, though potential visitors should hurry, as the proposed new High Speed (HS2) London to Birmingham line is currently scheduled to cut through this area. Once the tramway left Quainton Road, it then ran over the first of five level crossings and then ran adjacent to, but clearly separate from, the minor road heading south towards the A41. The way from Quainton Road to the location of the level crossing was clear to see, as was the line's course alongside the road. The clearly signposted footpath goes around the farm and soon rejoins the tramway's course. Between Waddesdon Road and Westcott (GR 720168), the path takes on several different forms, from being a concrete path at the beginning, to being a track on an open field at the end. Access ends at the Westcott Business Park

For the final stretch into Brill, the tramway would have followed close to the road almost all the way to the station, only diverging northwards a few hundred yards before arriving at the station's location itself. The only evidence of the railway's path today are a line of electricity poles that followed the line's course, the name of the Tramway Business Park, and a nearby house (originally, the station house) named Sleepers.

The station itself is about half a mile outside Brill because a relatively even gradient was required for the original horse power used when the line was originally conceived and since Brill is built on a hill, this was the most suitable and logical location for such a station.

The Peak Forest Tramway

Built under a 1794 Act of Parliament, the Peak Forest Tramway was planned to be just over 2 miles long, running from a canal basin at Chapel Milton to Lodes Knowle Quarry. However, the canal was shortened, terminating at Bugsworth (later Buxworth) Basin and the tramway was extended into Dove Holes Dale to serve the extensive quarries in this area. The completed canal and tramway, engineered by Benjamin Outram, opened for trade on Wednesday 31 August 1796 with an overall length of a little less than 6 miles. When the tramway was opened it was single track throughout its length, except for the Great Inclined Plane at Chapel-en-le-Frith and a short inclined plane at Lodes Knowle Quarry. The cast-iron rails were of L-section design, 1 yard long and weighing about 56lbs.

This tramway ran virtually unchanged through three centuries. Having been at the cutting edge of late eighteenth-century technology and having been extremely busy during the early part of the nineteenth century into the twentieth century, but as traffic declined due to rail and later road competition, it eventually became something of an anachronism. The last commercial gang of waggons to travel the complete length of the tramway occurred in 1922 when limestone from the quarry of S. Taylor Frith & Co. Ltd, in Dove Holes Dale, was taken down to Bugsworth Canal Basin. In 1924 the tramway between Dove Holes Dale and Chapel Milton was closed because the limestone and lime traffic was by then being transported by rail and road. All that remained was a little coal traffic to the mills between Bugsworth Canal Basin and Chapel Milton and some infrequent loads of cloth being sent down to Bugsworth Canal Basin from the mills.

In 1924 a commercial gang (comprised of some forty-five waggons) transported 113 tons of gritstone down to Bugsworth Canal Basin from Barren Clough Quarry to be used to build a cottage at Combs near Chapel-en-le-Frith. This was destined to be the last gang of waggons to use the tramway commercially and simultaneously the Barren Clough Quarry closed. The Peak Forest Tramway was formally closed in 1925. During 1927 and 1928 the tramway was dismantled with the scrap taken down

The Stodhart Tunnel on the Peak Forest Tramway before obliteration of the north portal in the 1940s. (Bertram Baxter collection)

to Bugsworth Canal Basin. In 1927 it was reported in *Edgar Allen News* that nearly 1,000 tons of old rails were stacked at Bugsworth Canal Basin awaiting disposal.

Today much of the line is easily walkable and accessible. At Dove Holes (GR 078780) the line split into several branches into different quarries, but much has been obliterated by later quarrying – just one minor branch survives, but the point where it reached the 'main line' is clearly identifiable, with complete rows of stone sleepers still in situ. Apart from a diversion round a flooded bridge, the line can be followed, albeit across some rough ground, to a point where it becomes parallel to the existing Buxton branch railway. Following this, the line reaches a spectacular ledge above the A6 road which runs into a gorge, although this is private and permission should be sought locally. After a short diversion, the top of the inclined plane is reached from a minor lane appropriately signposted 'Top o' the Plane'. Most of the plane is public and accessible, although the lower part is now incorporated into private gardens. Access is again possible for a short stretch through Chapel-en-le-Frith, but has been obliterated prior to reaching Stodhard Tunnel. As stated earlier, opened in 1796, this tunnel has a good case for being regarded as the oldest in the world. The north portal has long since gone due to road widening but the south portal lies next to the driveway of a residential home, and permission has been granted to view it in the past on request. The next section has been laid with

Trackbed of Peak Forest Tramway with sleeper blocks in situ west of Charley Lane, Chinley. (Author)

tarmac and is used for brake testing by the local firm Ferodo. From Charley Lane (GR 050817) the tramway forms an official path right through to Bugsworth Basin (GR 022821) where there was an interchange with the Peak Forest Canal. The basin was restored in recent years after decades of restoration by the Inland Waterways Protection Society and is now a scheduled ancient monument. There is much to see with minor canal arms now restored, sleeper blocks on both much in evidence and a second, more northerly, branch of the tramway reaching kilns on a two-arched bridge.

The Cromford & High Peak Railway

The Cromford & High Peak Railway was one of the last major tramways to be completed. This line, linking the Peak Forest Canal at Whaley Bridge with the Cromford Canal at High Peak Junction, opened throughout as a standard gauge line in 1831. Originally it was intended to be built as a canal, but height changes and potential water supply problems made a tramway more feasible. It was built using the 'inclines and level stretches' system, with the inclines all mechanically operated by stationary engines supplied by Benjamin Outram's firm at Butterley. Trials of locomotives on the route took place as early as December 1834, but it wasn't until 1860 that horses were replaced on runs of significant length. Indeed, as late as 1952 horses were still to be seen hauling waggons above the most westerly incline near Whaley Bridge. The line never really suited locomotive haulage; as well as gradients of up to 1 in 16, it abounded in sharp curves including the extraordinary Gotham Curve, with a radius of just 2½ chains – 55 yards! It is extraordinary to view the curve on a map let alone visit and walk round it.

With a walkable length of over 17 miles starting at the eastern end at Dowlow (GR 314560) to Parsley Hay (GR 147637) plus a further path at the western end running south from Whaley Bridge, at least two days are required to view all there is to see. We will have to settle for identifying some of the main features. Heading west from the workshops and offices that may still be viewed at High Peak Junction, the line passes under a bridge and straight up the first slope; this is the Sheep Pasture Incline, three-quarters of a mile straight uphill at a gradient of around 1 in 9.

Railway and canal interchange at Whaley Bridge, Cromford & High Peak Railway. (Bertram Baxter collection)

The engine house of the Middleton inclined plane, 708 yards long at a gradient of 1 in 8½, at Middleton Top was preserved as a visitor centre and the beam engines, once used to haul waggons, are occasionally demonstrated with compressed air. Samples of the original cast-iron rails may still be seen here. At Hopton there is a short, unlined tunnel followed by another inclined plane which gets steeper as you ascend; first a gentle 1 in 60, then 1 in 30 and finally a sharp 1 in 14. The embankment at Minninglow is spectacular too, a huge, lengthy stone structure, looking more like an old Roman wall than anything, built to hold a railway. Finally, before reaching Parsley Hay, another short tunnel with a carved emblem of a waggon above the portal is reached before a junction with the former (always locomotive-hauled) line through Tissington to Ashbourne, known as the Tissington Trail.

The Caldon Low Tramways
Although this area of Staffordshire is fascinating to explore, and indeed Caldon Low now has its later railway from Leek back in action in a new role as a preserved route, there is no doubt that it can leave the would-be explorer a little confused. That is because no fewer than four railways were built along an effectively parallel route from the Caldon Canal basin

A view of Froghall Wharf, Caldon Low Tramway. (Bertram Baxter collection)

at Froghall to the huge quarries at Caldon Low. The canal had reached Froghall by 1778 and to access the quarry, 3½ miles further but 670ft higher, a tramway was constructed and opened the same year. However, it was quickly recognised as being unsatisfactory – one contemporary account described it as 'very crooked, steep and uneven in its degrees of gradient in different parts'. By 1784 a second line was built, an improvement on the first, but with horses only able to pull one waggon

Caldon Low Tramways – trackbed on the fourth and last tramway. (Richard Lewis Collection)

at a time, it was inadequate for the growing level of traffic. The third railway, constructed in 1803, used horses on relatively level stretches but also gained the required height using four self-acting inclines. The line used flanged plates on stone blocks and therefore flangeless wheels. The fourth line, opened in 1847, now with flanged wheels on the waggons but sill using the same 3ft 6in gauge, was largely a series of self-acting, cable operated inclines, with no significant level stretches and therefore less requirement for horse power. This line, which was busy until the early years of the twentieth century, struggled on through the First World War and was finally closed in March 1920.

Starting at the picnic area at Froghall Wharf (GR 028477), where the canal tunnel and some well-preserved lime kilns may also be viewed, you see will see information boards with maps offering a choice of routes up or around the gradient towards the quarry. On the lowest part, an incline used by railways three and four, which crossed over and obliterated the line of railway two can be followed for some distance. Shortly afterwards you reach the A52 Whiston to Froghall Road and a section of the formation of railway three makes a delightful path through a wooded area. Slightly to the south of this point, a level section of railway two may also be followed for some distance. Proceeding to Upper Cotton, a fine bridge remains which carried the course of railway three over the formation of railway one. Also worth viewing, though do note that the west end is flooded to a depth of over 2ft, is the 330-yard tunnel constructed for the railway half a mile or so to the west of the quarries.

The Congleton Railway and Mow Cop Tramway

Almost certainly the least well known of the lines considered in this chapter, the Congleton Railway and the slightly later Mow Cop Tramway were both built to transport coal from Stonetrough Colliery, situated in the Biddulph Valley north of the small town of that name.

The Congleton Railway was opened around 1805, with the rails described in a contemporary account as 'oval or egg shaped', indicating that it was an edge railway rather than a plateway. It brought coal to a land wharf or landsale yard on Moss Road, a mile or so to the south east of Congleton. However, its opening unfortunately coincided with the bankruptcy of the colliery owners; it is believed that Stonetrough Colliery closed in 1807 and did not reopen until 1810, by which time it was too late for the railway, because according to Baxter it ceased to operate around 1809, although other sources have it clinging on into the 1840s. Similarly the line's gauge has never been accurately recorded; sources have varied from 2–4ft.

The Mow Cop Tramway was a slightly later venture; opening in 1842 at a 4–5ft gauge, it ran west and slightly north from the newly opened Tower Hill Colliery, adjacent to the older one at Stonecloough, on an almost straight run to reach a wharf on the Macclesfield Canal at Mow Cop. It included a now inaccessible tunnel of around 370 yards under a ridge of the Cop (though a party of enthusiasts apparently entered and explored it in January 2002). It is thought to have closed in 1887 when the collieries were bought by a rival owner and they were immediately shut down.

Although little has been done locally to provide information about the old lines, a surprising amount can be followed. Starting at the Congleton end, the formation can be picked up from a footpath off Tower Hill Road. It passes through woods, a short cutting and a fine long embankment close to Hillside Farm. Just north of the site of Stonecloough Colliery, now part of a farm, the two lines crossed, albeit at slightly different levels as the Congleton line had shut before the Mow Cop route opened. The Mow Cop line, outside of the tunnel area, is quite recognisable; first an incline can be seen crossing fields before the line becomes a rough track on its more level middle section. A further incline of around 1 in 8 lowered the tramway to reach the canal wharf at Mow Cop (GR 841580).

NORTH & MID WALES

The Nantlle Railway
Sometimes tramway aficionados argue about which was the first tunnel, the first public railway, and so on. But there is no dispute about the last tramway to operate. That honour goes to the quarry end of the Nantlle Railway, which remained worked by horses almost until closure in 1963. Authorised by an Act of 1825, the Nantlle Railway was up and running by 1828, taking slate and copper from mines and quarries in the Nantlle Valley to riverside quays in Caernarfon, close to the castle. The line was 9 miles in length and constructed at the unusual, 'neither narrow or standard' 3ft 6in gauge; this indicated a gauge chosen for its suitability for the traffic to be shipped and the local landscape, also given its date there were no other (standard or narrow gauge) lines to link up with. Running west from Nantlle to a station on the main road at Penygroes (where for a time a horse-drawn bus operated a service south to Porthmadog) the line then turned sharply to the north as it descended to Caernarfon.

Passengers were hauled from 1856; and then later, in 1865, the railway was absorbed into the Carnarvonshire Railway and later then by London & North Western Railway. The main part of its route, from Caernarfon to Penygroes, was rebuilt in 1867, in places on an adjacent alignment,

Tramway passing through Nantlle Slate Quarry. (Richard Lewis)

to single-track standard gauge main line standards to allow the operation of the Carnarvonshire Railway's steam-hauled trains through to Afon Wen. The lower valley section from Penygroes to Talysarn (where transshipment yards were laid out) was converted to standard gauge in 1872. The remainder of the line continued in use as a horse-drawn tramway linking Talysarn with several local quarries, and was operated as such by the LNWR. From 1923 it was operated by the London, Midland & Scottish Railway and from 1948 until 1963 by British Railways as far as the Pen-yr-Orsedd Quarry. The line was the only one to be operated by horses after nationalisation. One of the last pair of Nantlle horses, named 'Prince' and 'Corwen', attended the Festiniog Railway's 'Centenary of Steam' event in 1963, but after their retirement a tractor was used for the last year or so.

Parts of the Caernarfon to Dinas section of the Nantlle and Carnarvonshire Railways are now used jointly by the Welsh Highland Railway (WHR) and a cycle track, and thus easy to access. There are significant deviations between the 1828 and 1867 alignments, which can be traced in places. Notably, the Nantlle trackbed passes under the WHR by a short tunnel near Plas Dinas bridge, still standing over 130 years after abandonment, and an intact tunnel can be seen almost at right angles to the WHR at Coed Helen. It formed part of the Nantlle approach to the town, which crossed the Seiont downstream of the present crossing. The Nantlle's original terminus premises survive within the 'Island Site' near Caernarfon station. Much of the eastern end of the route is traceable today as far as the easterly terminus at Penyrorsedd Quarry.

Inclines and railway buildings on the Nantlle Railway. (Bertram Baxter collection)

A further enterprise, Dorothea Quarry, also used the Nantlle Railway to dispatch slate from 1829 until 1959. Of note here were two large structures, known as pyramids; these served as bases for the chain inclines and allowed the waste rock to be tipped behind. Tunnels were built under them to allow the tramway to pass through.

The Talyllyn Railway

A day out on the Talyllyn combines a trip on Britain's oldest preserved railway with a chance to explore its much less well-known former horse-drawn upper section. Unlike its neighbour and sharer of the 2ft 3in gauge, the Corris Railway and the Festiniog Railway to the north, the lower part of the Talyllyn was locomotive hauled from the start. Passenger services originally only ran as far as Abergynolwen – but far more important was the slate traffic, carried down via a series of inclines and level sections from a huge quarry at Bryn Eglws to Nant Gwernol. Preservationists reopened the line to Nant Gwernol for passenger trains in 1976.

Underground working began in the early 1840s and by 1847 the quarry was being worked by local landowner John Pughe. The finished slates were sent by packhorse and then riverboat to reach the harbour at Aberdovey and then finally loaded into seagoing vessels, a complex and expensive transportation arrangement which limited the quarry's output. In January 1864 the Aberdovey Slate Company was formed which leased the land, including Bryn Eglwys, from the landowner, and in 1865 this company earmarked money for the construction of a narrow gauge railway connecting the quarry with the port of Aberdyfi, though the route was shortened once alternative facilities became available at Tywyn.

Our exploration starts at the far end of Nant Gwernol station, where we straightaway start to ascend our first cable-hauled incline, the Alltwyllt. Here were stables for the horses and the ruins of a building that held the cables remain, as does a pair of rails restored to position in order to give a clear idea of how the lines climbed up and over the head of the incline. Once up we can enjoy a delightful level section, high on a ledge, level with the tops of trees from the valley below. Continuing on, we reach the site of the next incline, the Cantrybedd, which lifted the rails to the first quarries at an altitude of around 700ft. Anthony Burton, in his 1985 book

Restored rails at the top of the Alltwyllt incline above Nant Gwernol, Talyllyn Railway. (Author)

Walking the Line, described clambering onto and walking up this incline as being a straightforward matter, but unfortunately soon afterwards a landslip blocked the top end and it is now totally overgrown and inaccessible. A somewhat roundabout route up a zig-zag but well-signposted path serves as an alternative and it is possible to explore further level stretches, taking the explorer past and beyond the former quarry buildings which lead to further inclines and minor routes. Make sure your route brings you back to Nant Gwernol or Abergynolwen in time for the last train!

The Penrhyn Railway

The Penrhyn Railway is thought to be the earliest narrow gauge line of any length in North Wales. The Penrhyn Quarry Railway dates back to 1801 when Lord Penrhyn's land agent Benjamin Wyatt designed a narrow gauge railway to link Penrhyn slate quarries at Bethesda with Port Penrhyn at Bangor, North Wales, a distance of some 6 miles. Wyatt was able to make use of a short section of existent track then known as the Llandegai Tramway constructed in 1798 to link Port Penrhyn with a flint mill near Llandegai village. The railway took a very direct route and consisted of four

Penrhyn Railway – the harbour at Port Penrhyn with track visible either side of the bridge. (Bertram Baxter collection)

Locomotive and shed at Penrhyn Railway. The building at the left rear of the photograph was the line's former stables. (Penrhyn Railway collection)

level plains divided by three inclines, the first at Maesgeirchen near Bangor, the second at Dinas near Tregarth and the third at Tanysgafell known as Tyn-y-Clwt incline. The railway was completed in 1801 and featured iron edge rails 3ft in length and supported on slate and stone blocks. The gauge was measured from rail centre to centre which gave a gauge measurement of 2ft. However, when the measurement was taken from inside the rails, Penrhyn Quarries ended up with the rather unusual gauge of 1ft 10¾in, a gauge that was adhered to until closure in the 1960s.

Following the opening of the Chester & Holyhead route, the Penrhyn had a close neighbour in the Port Penrhyn line which linked the main line with the harbour of that name and which was privately owned and ran for its whole length through the estate of Lord Penrhyn. The Bethesda line ran happily and profitably as a tramroad for over seventy years, but eventually, in 1877, locomotives were introduced and a slightly amended route was laid out to bypass the inclined planes. One of the most profitable of narrow gauge lines, tiny engines were to be seen hauling slate down to the harbour and returning back up with the empties for over eighty years. Locals demanded that the Penrhyn ran a passenger service, but were rebuffed and eventually in 1884 the LNWR built a conventional standard gauge line from Bethesda to Bangor on a nearby, and in places parallel, route.

Turning back to the Penrhyn, the line remained much as it was until its closure in July 1962. The railway officially closed to traffic on the 24 July 1962; however, the locomotive Blanche worked several slate runs after this date before being loaded onto a lorry at Felin Fawr in December 1963, destined for Porthmadog. The Port Penrhyn line succumbed soon after, closing in March 1963.

The 6 miles of track between Felin Fawr works at Bethesda and Port Penrhyn was also destined for the Festiniog Railway and was eventually lifted in 1965. By this time the Penrhyn estate had been bequeathed to the National Trust, and this helped the preservation of much of the old line. A section of just over 2 miles in length south from Bangor as far as Glasinfryn (GRs 592726 to 587692) is now designated an official path and is popular with both walkers and cyclists, who can then continue on towards Bethesda on a short section of the former LNWR line. It is worth also noting a preservation society on the Penrhyn Quarry Railway is slowly working towards restoration, with work on a section at Bethesda currently in progress.

The Glyn Valley Tramway

The Glyn Valley Tramway was originally a horse-drawn line, connecting Chirk with Glyn Ceiriog in Denbighshire. The line was the only roadside tramway in Wales and had a unique gauge of 2ft 4½in. The total length of the line was 8¼ miles, 6½ miles of which were worked by passenger trains, the remainder serving a large granite quarry and several minor slate quarries. The railway was built to connect the quarries at Glyn Ceriog with the Shropshire Union Canal at Chirk. An Act of Parliament in 1870 incorporated the Glyn Valley Tramway, which allowed the company to build a narrow gauge tramway from the canal at Chirk Bank to the Cambrian Slate Quarries. This initial line was opened in 1873, and was worked by horse and gravity traction. Both passenger and freight traffic was carried from that year. In 1885 additional parliamentary powers were obtained to abandon the Quinta Tramway section between Pontfaen and Chirk Bank, replacing it with a new line from Pontfaen to the Great Western Railway's Chirk station. A 2-mile extension was also authorised from Glyn to the quarries around Pandy. Rebuilding of the line was undertaken with steam locomotives borrowed from the Snailbeach District Railways. The new line was opened for freight traffic in 1888 and to passengers in 1891, operated by steam locomotives purchased from Beyer Peacock in Manchester.

Due to its setting alongside the B4500, the trackbed can be followed quite easily for much of its distance. A number of features also survive to be viewed, including the former waiting room at Pontfadog and a sizeable

Replica track and shed on the Glyn Valley Tramway today. (Richard Lewis)

Bridge over Glyn Valley Tramway. (Richard Lewis)

tract of land at Glyn Ceiriog, the former Coal Wharf. Most recently, one of two local preservation groups has secured from Wrexham Borough Council a lease over the former locomotive shed and yard at Glyn Ceiriog on which work is already in progress to restore and convert it to a Tramway & Industrial Heritage Centre for the Ceiriog Valley.

NORTH-WEST ENGLAND AND SCOTLAND

The Storeton Tramway

This was a single-track, standard gauge railway which was used to transport stone from three quarries at Storeton to Bromborough Pool. From there it was taken by barge to Birkenhead and Liverpool to be used in the construction of buildings. Before the railway was built, horse-drawn carts were used on the local roads.

It may be noted that the Storeton was one of the last horse-drawn lines to open. The idea of constructing such a railway in the locality dated back to the late 1820s, when in 1828 George Stephenson visited the quarries. He was looking for stone to use for construction of the Sankey Viaduct on the Liverpool & Manchester Railway, though the tramway was not completed in time to serve that purpose. Construction of the Storeton line began in April 1837 and was completed in August 1838 at a cost of £12,000, using stone blocks bought second hand from the Liverpool & Manchester Railway. The original name was the Stourton Railway (original spelling of village). In the quarry's latter years it was known as Storeton Quarries Tramway then as merely the Storeton Tramway. Nowadays it is locally known as the 'waggon line'.

As noted above, the line serviced three quarries: Storeton North, Storeton South and Jackie's Wood Quarry, which was on the east side of Mount Road. It started at the North Quarry, then past the South Quarry, over Rest Hill Road, through Hancock's Wood and into a 60-yard tunnel under Mount Road. It emerged in Jackie's Wood Quarry. It then passed across Bracken Lane, Cross Lane and Church Road (near to St Andrew's Church) and onto the quay at Bromborough Pool. From the quarries to Mount Road the waggons were hauled by horses, but from then on they were propelled by gravity at speeds of up to 20mph, the whole journey only taking around thirty minutes. Horses provided the power for the return journey at a more sedate speed. By the 1890s quarrying stopped at the North Quarry but the others remained in operation into the early years of the twentieth century. The last waggon load set out from Bromborough in 1905, and the tramway was then abandoned. All three quarries were eventually infilled by spoil dug out during construction of the Mersey Tunnels.

During the Second World War, the Mount Road Tunnel was converted into an air-raid shelter by a local man, Mr Jacques, who fitted bunks and a protective door. Later stone excavations at this site caused a collapse and it became two shorter tunnels. You can still see the cutting which approaches the west entrance to the tunnel. Parts of the cutting to the north quarry are still visible as are a number of stone sleeper blocks. These blocks, notable for having as many as four bolt holes (perhaps due to having been used twice) have in places been incorporated into walls around the area.

The Walton Summit Plateway

A number of tramways were constructed around the end of the eighteenth century to temporarily link isolated sections of canal. Other examples include those at Marple on the Peak Forest Canal and at Caen Hill near Devizes on the Kennet & Avon Canal, both of which were eventually replaced, as always intended, by long flights of locks. The Walton Summit Plateway, however, was never replaced, no aqueduct was built across the River Ribble and the two sections of the Lancaster Canal with which it linked remained permanently separate. The original plan foresaw an impressive stone aqueduct across the river and up to thirty-two locks to complete the route, but instead, the canal company constructed a tramroad to link the two halves and allow revenue traffic to start flowing. Construction took three years before opening in 1795.

The 5-mile-long tramroad comprised a double-track 4ft 3in gauge plateway except for a short section of single track through a tunnel under Fishergate in Preston, just south of the canal basin. As suggested by the name, the iron rails were 'L' shaped in section and were spiked to large limestone blocks; the wheels on the waggons were not flanged and were kept on the track by the vertical section of the rails. As was common on early 'railway' systems, the waggons could be privately owned by the hauliers themselves (known locally as halers), who paid the company a toll to use the tramroad. The last haler to work the tramroad, John Procter, apparently walked the 10-mile return journey twice a day for thirty-two years; implying that he walked or rode an amazing 200,000 miles during his career on the tramroad.

In 1813, estimates were prepared to replace the tramroad by a canal but the cost of £160,000 was too much for the company at the time. In 1837 the new Bolton & Preston Railway leased the tramroad as a potential alternative route into Preston that avoided the rival North Union Railway. However, a merger was concluded between the two parties before this proved necessary. This created a railhead for Wigan coal in Preston and removed the *raison d'être* of the tramroad.

Although the North Union wanted to close the tramroad immediately the canal company objected and they were forced to maintain it in an increasingly decrepit state until an 1864 Act allowed closure of the tramroad between Preston and Bamber Bridge. In 1872, a land exchange

Trackbed of Walton Summit Plateway south of Preston – possibly Britain's oldest Railway Path. (Author)

between Preston Corporation and the railway saw the formation between Preston and Carr Wood pass into municipal ownership. This section, including the tramroad bridge over the River Ribble, was turned into a footpath, in which form it remains to the present day. It therefore has a clear claim to be Britain's first 'railway path'. A further act in 1879 enabled the last part of the tramroad between Bamber Bridge and Walton Summit, to be closed. The north end of the canal was eventually sold to the London & North Western Railway and the Lancaster Canal Company was wound up at the beginning of 1886.

Today the best place to join the tramway is the top part of Avenham Park in Preston, where a footpath follows the course of the former incline down to the River Ribble. The tramroad crossed the Ribble on a timber trestle bridge nearly 150 yards long, which outlived the tramroad by nearly a hundred years and was only replaced by a pre-cast concrete structure built to the same design in 1965. After the bridge, the tramway continued along a delightful tree-lined embankment to Penwortham

Replica bridge over River Ribble at Preston on the Walton Summit Plateway. (Author)

Mill, before rising to Walton Summit on another incline. There may just be the odd stone sleeper still in situ, but most that were left have now been removed – some are now features in adjacent gardens! The 'official' tramway path ends amongst modern housing at Limekiln Farm, though a further section is walkable just east of the modern A6 motorway link road at Bamber Bridge. The site of the canal/tramway exchange at Walton Summit (GR approx. 582247) is marked only by a grassy mound with no information board or other feature to identify it.

The Lord Carlisle's Railway

Although the Brampton Railway (or Lord Carlisle's Railway) probably had its origins in a short wooden waggonway at Tindale Fell Colliery in about 1776, the main line westwards wasn't built until 1798, with the first waggon of coal being horse-hauled to Brampton in April 1799. No Act of Parliament was obtained as the vast majority of the system was built by Lord Carlisle on his own land. By 1808 it had been relaid with cast-iron and wrought-iron rails, it being the first application of the latter in a day-to-day commercial way.

In 1836 a horse-worked passenger service was introduced when the track was realigned to meet up with the Newcastle & Carlisle Railway (N&CR) at Brampton Junction. The passenger service ceased in 1881 but in 1913 the NER took over the branch, relaid the track and introduced a steam-worked passenger service. The NER suspended passenger trains between 1917 and 1920 and the LNER withdrew the service for good in 1923. Complete closure came at the end of 1923 and the following year the track was lifted. These lines have been called at different periods the Tindale Fell Railway, the Midgeholme Railway, the Hartleyburn & Brampton Railway and simply the Brampton Railway. It also became one of the first non-Stephenson railways to convert and adopt the standard gauge of 4ft 8½in. The year 1836 saw conversion to locomotive power, with the famous *Rocket* (purchased from the Liverpool & Manchester Railway) in use from the following year, though it proved unsuitable for the heavy loads that needed to be hauled. In 1947 the mines and railway came under the control of the National Coal Board but six years later, after being in use for 155 years, mining ceased and the railway closed.

The Brampton Railway, known locally as the 'Dandy Line', began at the former Brampton Town station (GR 538611) and, now an official path throughout, climbs gently for a mile and a quarter to Brampton Junction

Trackbed on Lord Carlisle's Railway east of Hallbankgate. (Author)

(GR 550600) this being the only section to have a regular passenger service. The original eighteenth-century alignment ran to the north-east of the later line, and some short pieces of cutting may still be made out here. From Brampton Junction (GR 550600) it headed east, though the trackbed is no longer accessible here and after a mile ascended by a self-acting inclined plane from Kirkhouse (GR 566598) to Planehead with gradients varying from 1 in 22 to 1 in 17½ and mostly just three rails each a standard gauge apart, with a division into two separate 'lines' only at the central passing place. A level crossing carried the line over the B6292 at Hallbankgate (now A689) and a branch to Blacksyke, Gairs and Howgill then diverged to the south. Official access can be resumed here, continuing through Bluegate to Tindale (GR 617593), where there were smelting works and collieries. Turning south-east towards Midgeholme (GR 642588), the line ran for about a mile along a high embankment made in 1824 crossing the valley which divides Cumberland from Northumberland. The line then skirted the northern escarpment of Hartleyburn Common with another level crossing (GR 655584) taking it over the A689 at Haltonleagate shortly after which public access to the line ends. The line terminated at Hallbankgate until an 1849 extension reached Lambley (GR 674581), and a junction with the Alston line, upon the latter line's opening in 1852.

The Edinburgh & Dalkeith Railway

The Edinburgh & Dalkeith Railway was a pioneering wrought-iron railed 4ft 6in gauge horse-drawn line. Engineered by James Jardine, it was originally built to transport coal from the Dalkeith area into the city centre, opening on 4 July 1831, with a branch to Fisherrow Harbour at Musselburgh opening just a few months later. The following year a passenger service was introduced which, most unusually, proved to be more popular and profitable than the freight service, though fares starting at as little as 3*d* for a return trip would also have helped. At first a converted stage coach was used, but as its popularity grew all kinds of waggons were pressed into service. From 1832 to 1845 the railway carried 200,000 to 300,000 passengers per year – more per mile than the Liverpool & Manchester Railway. The line was bought by the North British Railway in 1845 and within two years was a standard gauge steam-hauled route forming part of Edinburgh's suburban network.

Locally always known as the 'innocent railway', a number of explanations have been put forward for this peculiar name. Whether simply because horse haulage was old fashioned, or seemingly safer than the apparently dangerous steam locomotives it is difficult from

South Portal of St Leonard's Tunnel on the Edinburgh & Dalkeith Railway. (Phillip Earnshaw)

this distance to know for sure. The final St Leonards section included a gravity-operated incline which passed through a 572-yard tunnel lit by gas lamps. The incline had a gradient of 1 in 30 and was worked by a stationary steam winding engine. A viaduct at Thornybank, Dalkeith, was demolished in the 1960s. The tunnel, thought to be Scotland's earliest, has an unusual feel when walking through it due to the gradient. Part of the line is about to be reused as part of the revived northern section of the 'Waverley Route' from the Borders, but a 2¾-mile section (GR 269727 – 312725) from Holyrood Park Road in central Edinburgh to Brunstane including St Leonards Tunnel is now a popular footpath and cycle route into the city centre.

The Tranent to Cockenzie Waggonway

The Tranent to Cockenzie Waggonway was the first railway to be built in Scotland, opening in 1722. Following local landowner the 5th Earl of Wintoun's support of the first Jacobite Rising in 1715, his estates were forfeited to the Crown and subsequently sold to the York Buildings Company of London in 1719. This company had great difficulties in managing the estate from London and so encouraged local tenants to improve the lands. Cockenzie's primitive harbour was reconstructed, and, in order to carry the Tranent coal in greater quantities to Cockenzie, a primitive horse-operated wooden railed waggonway was built. It was 2½ miles long and connected two small towns in East Lothian, transporting coal from the pit heads at Tranent, including Fleets Colliery, to Cockenzie Harbour via Meadowmill. Horse-drawn waggons were used which held 2 tons of coal. On the return journey the horses would pull five empty waggons back to Tranent, making around three round trips per day. The line ran close to the site of the Battle of Prestonpans (1745) and it has been said that the first use of a railway in warfare occurred here as is it is possible that soldiers were carried to the battleground in the waggons.

Sleeper blocks in situ at Cockenzie Harbour – terminus of the Tranent–Cockenzie Railway, Scotland's oldest. (Bertram Baxter collection)

The waggonway operated effectively for no fewer than 150 years until about 1880 when a coal merchant named James Waldie took over the lease of the Tranent collieries and the waggonway. The waggonway was then rebuilt as a standard gauge railway with steam locomotives, and a junction was made with the North British Railway at Meadowmill. Twenty years later, James Waldie and some other leading East Lothian coalmasters combined to form the Edinburgh Collieries Co. Ltd. The old Tranent to Cockenzie Waggonway, now a busy steam railway, was once again extended to Fleets Colliery. The old waggonway, suitably modernised, continued to carry coal down to the main line railway at Meadowmill, until just before the closure of Fleets Colliery in 1959. This meant that parts of the route were used as a railway for nearly 240 years. A modern railway nearby brought coal into Cockenzie until the late 1980s, but only to supply the nearby power station.

There is still much to be seen today of this line. Almost the whole of the route of the 1722 waggonway is clearly visible, and indeed most of its length is used as a public path by walkers, cyclists, and horse-riders today, though no information board or other historical background has been provided. At Cockenzie Harbour a few old stone sleepers are still in position and may be viewed amonsgst or underneath the vehicles parked on the quayside.

YORKSHIRE

The Silkstone Railway

Locally known as the 'waggonway', the Silkstone Railway was built in 1809 by the Barnsley Canal Navigation Company who had been granted an Act of Parliament for its construction the previous year. This railway was built to transport coal from the collieries in the Silkstone Valley 2½ miles from Silkstone Cross to Barnby Basin, Cawthorne, the terminus of the canal. It was extended in the early 1830s when one Robert C. Clarke, colliery owner of Noblethorpe Hall, who was sinking a new colliery at Moor End near Silkstone Common to exploit the reserves of coal in the Dove Valley, had the problem of getting the coal to the canal in the Silkstone Valley. This was solved by building an inclined plane to bring the waggons of coal up from Moor End, which was achieved by the use of a steam engine (Black Horse Engine) which pulled the waggons to the top of the hill at Silkstone Common. North of here was Black Horse Tunnel (now blocked up but with a plaque marking the site of one portal) under the later Penistone to Barnsley railway line and adjacent main road. On the north side of the tunnel there was a self-acting inclined plane. This arrangement continued until the line had to bow to locomotive-hauled competition and ceased operation some time in the 1860s.

In 1998, The Silkstone Waggonway Restoration Group was formed to look at ways of restoring some features of the waggonway. The line is instantly recognisable as a tramroad, with large numbers of stone sleeper blocks, to which the iron rails where bolted, still in place. The majority of these sleeper blocks were, unusually, placed at 45-degree angles to give a 'diamond' appearance. A short length of waggonway was replaced on its original route at Silkstone Cross, and a replica waggon was added later. A further waggon has been replaced on trackbed on the eastern side of Silkstone village outside a garden centre. As the line heads down the valley, it becomes a particularly quiet and pleasant walk away from the busy roads. Walking on, the trail takes you to the group of cottages called Barnby Furnace, which smelted iron stone using charcoal. A path to the right crosses Furnace Bridge and leads to Higham. In the past this area was served by a railway branch line built in the 1850s to collieries in the area, a direct competitor to the waggonway which must surely have sealed its fate. The terminus at Barnby Basin shows little of its past; the canal here having been abandoned in 1893 with only the faintest of traces remaining.

Replica chaldron waggon in Silkstone Village at Silkstone Railway. (Author)

The Heck Bridge & Wentbridge Railway

The Heck Bridge & Wentbridge Railway was laid to a gauge of 3ft 6in on stone sleeper blocks. There remains some doubt about whether it was laid as a plateway or edge way, given its date, the latter is considered more likely. It opened in 1827 but funds ran out after two years, much more than expected having been spent on the canal basin, and though it was authorised to be sold in 1833, it struggled on before finally closing in 1840. It was built to carry limestone from quarries in the Went Valley to the Knottingley & Goole Canal (Aire & Calder Navigation) at Heck. Given that the railway was abandoned over 170 years ago, it is perhaps surprising that so much survives.

Heck Basin (GR 584208) still exists on the Aire & Calder Navigation and is now the headquarters of a boat club. There is very little evidence here these days of any transport exchange infrastructure. From the basin the single line headed south along the eastern side of Heck Lane, identifiable as a wide grassy verge, for just over a mile. After this point the line has been completely obliterated for some distance; it once crossed the erstwhile Hull & Barnsley Railway at what would become the north end

Bridge carrying former Heck & Wentbridge Railway over a stream at Kirk Smeaton. (Author)

of Kirk Smeaton station yard (situated in Little Smeaton) and then entered a short cutting, the only substantial one on the line. It is therefore best to omit this stretch and to make for Kirk Smeaton itself. Here, below the church can be seen the remains of a small but well-constructed bridge that carried the line over what was once a millstream. Just west of here, a public footpath can be picked up which follows the course of the line west of Kirk Smeaton, passing three small quarries along the south bank of the River Went. The path ends where the realigned A1 dual-carriageway bridges the river, close to the site of Wentbridge Quarry, located on the border of West and North Yorks. A short branch led to Brockendale Quarry (GR 5112171) whilst the 'main line' ended at Wentbridge Quarry (GR 495171), some 4 miles south of Pontefract.

The Aberford Railway

Some of the most difficult railways in Great Britain about which to obtain precise information are those which have been built privately, without statutory powers, and therefore without needing any Board of Trade or Ministry of Transport inspection. One such line is the Aberford Railway, extending from Garforth northward to the village of Aberford on the Great North Road.

Trackbed of Garforth to Aberford Railway approaching Aberford. (Author)

The line as surveyed by William Harker and William Walker, and built by Robert Kirkup opened in 1836 (possibly 1835) and had a continuous run dropping 100ft from Garforth to Aberford. The steepest point was a 1 in 72 bank down from the Sisters Pit, compared to the shallowest gradient of 1 in 440 near Isabella. The continuous run allowed for gravity working down to Aberford, and horse working back up to Garforth. One peculiarity of this line is that virtually none of the required 10,000 stone blocks have been found; it appears that for some reason wooden sleepers may have been used instead. There are a small number of stone sleeper blocks currently located under turf at the Aberford terminus, but these appear to be from an even older railway from Parlington Colliery to Aberford. Such a line would have become defunct with the closure of Parlington Colliery in 1822.

Between February 1838 and February 1839, the Aberford Railway recorded a total distance of 2,300 miles travelled. This works out at about seventeen or eighteen journeys (of both coal and passenger traffic) a week, making it apparently much less busy than many other similar lines. Early passengers were carried on a horse-drawn waggon known as the 'High Flyer'. Built by the colliery carpenters who had little coach-building experience, the waggon was notably spartan. Wooden cross benches were used for seats, and lighting was supplied by three small windows on either side. A dandy cart was also attached behind the 'High Flyer'. For the journey to Aberford, the train only needed horse haulage up the bank from Sisters Yard. The horse was then uncoupled, and was trained to nimbly step onto the dandy cart as it passed down the hill towards Aberford. Locally known as the 'Aberford Fly Line', the line was converted to locomotive operation in 1870 and closed to all traffic in 1924.

Our exploration of what remains starts in Garforth (GR 407336) on Ash Lane beside the main A642 road. The course of the tramroad can easily be picked up as a straight footpath on a low embankment heading north. At Hawk's Nest the Fly Line passes under the busy M1 but soon the sound of traffic fades and one is deep in woodland. Curving north-east, the line passes Parlington Hall where there was a private gasworks and coal staithe, and domestic servants would alight, returning from visits to Garforth. Soon the line reaches Dark Arch. Close on 100 yards long, it has all the appearance of a railway tunnel but predates the line by twenty years. The arch was created when the lawn of Parlington Hall was extended to hide coal traffic that passed along Parlington Lane from pits to the west. A sunken fence, or ha-ha, between lawn and parkland prevented deer straying over and when it proved impractical to take the railway through the tunnel the ha-ha provided a ready-made cutting. A second bridge,

'The Light Arch' bridge over Garforth to Aberford Railway. (Author)

known as the 'Light Arch', crosses the line then it is little more than half a mile into Aberford (GR 419281). The walls of coal staithes above the depot yard can still be seen here. From Aberford buses are available to return weary tramway explorers back to Leeds or other local destinations.

The Whitby & Pickering Railway (Grosmont)

This is a delightful line where the tramway explorer can combine the pleasure of a walk with a steam-hauled return trip on a preserved railway. The North Yorkshire Moors Railway was first opened in 1836 as the Whitby & Pickering Railway. The railway was planned in 1831 by George Stephenson as a means of opening up trade routes inland from the then important seaport of Whitby. The three main achievements were cutting a 120-yard tunnel through rock at Grosmont, constructing a rope-worked incline system at Beck Hole and traversing the marshy and deep Fen Bog using a bed of timber and sheep fleeces. The tunnel was designed by Frederick Swanwick, an assistant to Stephenson. However, his choice of expensive castellated entrances was much to the distaste of the railway's owners. It is now believed to be one of the oldest walkable railway tunnels in the world. In its first year of operation, the railway carried 10,000 tons of stone from Grosmont to Whitby, as well as 6,000 passengers who paid a fare of 1s to sit on the roof of a coach, or 1s 3d to sit inside. It took two and a half hours to travel from Whitby to Pickering.

In 1845 the railway was acquired by the York & North Midland Railway who re-engineered the line to allow the use of steam locomotives. They also constructed the permanent stations and other structures along the line which still remain today. The Beck Hole Incline was re-equipped with a steam-powered stationary engine and iron rope. Beck Hole was served by the original Whitby to Pickering railway line until 1864, when a hauling line snapped and a carriage plunged down the original incline, killing two of the occupants. Steam locomotives could not operate on the Beck Hole incline; so in the early 1860s the North Eastern Railway started construction of an alternate route which opened in 1865; this is the route which is still in use today.

Starting at Grosmont – headquarters of the North Yorkshire Moors Railway – which is served by the Whitby to Middlesbrough line, we can

Track at Beck Hole, south of Grosmont. (Bertram Baxter collection)

Tramway (left) and modern railway tunnels south of Grosmont. (Author)

first enjoy a walk through the original tunnel – though this is now a 'dead end' with access only to the preserved line's engine sheds. Continuing south, a well-signposted footpath takes us over the tunnel and onto the west side of the preserved line. Known as the 'Historical Rail Trail' the route continues south to the incline at Beck Hole, with some missing bridges now replaced by narrow steel structures bolted onto the original stone abutments. At Goathland the official trail ends and a steam powered trip back to Grosmont may be enjoyed. However, the original line remains a public path for a further 1½ miles to Moorgates, just north of the junction between old and new routes.

Amongst other, shorter lines worth exploring in Yorkshire is the Skipton Tramway, taking limestone from the Earl of Thanet's quarries past the castle to the Canal Spur in Skipton and the New Hall Tramway near Wakefield, possibly the location of the first tramway tunnel. Do not forget the Middleton Railway in Leeds either, a ride can be accompanied by a look at the original route and some fascinating artefacts.

NORTH-EAST ENGLAND

The Waskerley Way

Although a very early conversion to locomotive haulage, this line retains to this day a very 'tramroad' feel as it crosses some remote and inhospitable countryside. It was promoted by the Stanhope & Tyne Railway, and aimed to bring limestone and iron from quarries above Stanhope to the port at South Shields. Opened throughout by 1834 the line featured a number of inclined planes, including the noted Nanny Mayor's incline (named after a local innkeeper), enabling the line to go down and back up the huge gorge

Stockton & Darlington Railway milepost on the Waskerley line. (Author)

Trackbed of Waskerley Way with the Sheepfold line coming in from the left. (Author)

at Hownes Gill. Financial problems ensued despite the line being very busy with freight; a passenger service down to Stanhope was very short lived and there were a number of changes of ownership until it was purchased by the Stockton & Darlington Railway in 1845. The Stockton & Darlington constructed a new route, bypassing Nanny Mayor's incline with a huge viaduct at Hownes Gill. The date of conversion to locomotive haulage is not entirely clear, though it would have been no later than 1846 when a locomotive shed was constructed at Waskerley.

The entire route (GR 099493 – 993405) including the later diversion from the terminus at Crawley above Stanhope to Burnhill Junction between Crook and Consett may be followed, as can a portion of the original route into Hownes Gill. As you cross the moor the landscape is unquestionably bleak, with few trees and extensive views when clear. Passing Parkend, where tea and sustenance may be available in the former station building, a branch can be explored which heads off north-west towards quarries at Sheepfold. When the author explored this line in 2007 the surface was rather rough and stony but it may well have improved since then as it is now part of the National Cycle Network.

After Parkend, the line, hugging the contours, turns due east towards Waskerley. Here the original and 1850s diversion parted ways. Although never carrying horse-drawn traffic, if nearby it would be a shame to omit a crossing of Hownes Gill Viaduct. At 730ft (220m) long and 150ft (45m) high it is a giant amongst viaducts, and the sense of being above the tops of huge trees can be a little unnerving, particularly if they are swaying backwards and forwards on a breezy day. For those wanting to follow the original route, the upper two-thirds of Nanny Mayor's incline is accessible, but the footpath then deviates away to the west before curving back round where a short further section of track is accessible. From Whitehall, where old and new routes join or Burnhill Junction it is then best to proceed north towards Consett where onwards transport is available.

The Tanfield Railway

The Tanfield Railway was originally built to transport coal from the collieries of County Durham, to various staithes on the southern bank of the River Tyne, for onward transport in colliers (bulk coal carrying ships). The oldest part of the original Tanfield Railway, located to the north-east of the present heritage line, in the Lobley Hill area, dated from 1647, and was in continuous use for over 315 years, quite possibly a world record, until final closure in 1964. Originally a wooden-railed horse-drawn waggonway, conversion to a conventional steel-railed railway was completed by 1840 as far as Tanfield Moor Colliery. In 1881 the railway was converted to steam locomotive operation, becoming part of the North Eastern Railway.

Its great monument, the Causey Arch, is claimed to be the oldest railway bridge in the world and was reckoned to be the largest civil engineering project carried out in Britain since Roman times. It was built by a local stonemason, Ralph Wood, who worried so much about the structure that he sadly took his own life. It was built to carry a secondary branch from the route of the now preserved line, to a site known as Dawson's Drift. Built between 1725 and 1727, at 150ft (46m) long and 80ft (24m) high, it was the largest single-span bridge in Britain, and remained so for thirty years. After railway activity stopped, the bridge quietly mouldered for almost 200 years until it was restored by Durham County Council in the 1980s. The route and structures of the oldest section of what now forms the preserved part of the line, between Sunniside and Causey, date from 1725, and thus has a legitimate claim to be the world's oldest working railway.

Our walk starts at the southern end of the 'preserved' Tanfield Railway at East Tanfield station, not far from Beamish Hall, former home of the Shaftoe family – one of whom, Bobby Shaftoe, became the subject of a nursery rhyme. From East Tanfield we follow one of several waggonways

Decking at top of the Causey Arch. (Author)

that led to Causey Arch. Horses pulled waggons holding 4 tons of coal along this route above the increasingly steep slopes of the Causey Gill gorge – in many places embankments had to be built to ensure a level route for the wooden rails. Today it is a peaceful path but in its short heyday, from 1725 to the 1740s, the track saw hundreds of waggons, each only 50 yards apart, carry their loads of coal towards the bridge. After crossing the arch, a path takes you down into the gorge where you can admire the arch from below and you can see where the Causey Burn was diverted through culverts to enable the embankments to be constructed. After reaching a car park and picnic area, a diversion must be followed to Andrews House station. From this point the footpath again runs parallel to the preserved line, passing the locomotive shed and museum before reaching the 'end of the line' at Sunniside. From here, the walker has the line to his or her self, and descends towards the Tyne by means of three inclines. The line passes Watergate Forest Park before entering more urban surroundings, ending rather anonymously next to a slip road off the A1 after the final, 1 in 18, Lobley Hill incline (GR 232614).

The Wylam Waggonway
A line of great historical significance, particularly in terms of locomotive construction, the line opened in 1748 as a 5ft gauge wooden waggonway

(with originally timber rails 3½in wide and 4½in deep attached to stone sleepers at 18in intervals) running from Wylam Colliery to Lemington, from where the coal was taken down the River Tyne on flat-bottomed boats called keels to be loaded on the large coal ships further down the river. A look at a current map shows the River Tyne now running closer to Blaydon and some distance south of where the original staithes would have been; its course having long since been altered to avoid a large loop at Lemington. The line had a switchback profile, which meant that horses had to haul fully laden waggons up as well as down the gradients; as a result much smaller loads could be hauled by each horse than on other such routes. In 1808 wooden rails were replaced by iron rails and shortly afterwards Wylam Colliery's manager William Hedley started to experiment with locomotives to haul the waggons, most notably the *Puffing Billy* and the *Wylam Dilly*. Initially these were four-wheelers but this caused extensive damage to the track and they were rebuilt with eight wheels on two bogies. Both are preserved but, perhaps unfortunately,

Wylam waggonway, now part of the National Cycle Network. (Author)

neither remained local; *Puffing Billy* of 1813 is at the Science Museum in London whilst *Wylam Dilly* of 1814 is at the Royal Scottish Museum in Edinburgh. This is generally considered to be the first commercially viable use of steam traction. The line continued to be used in this fashion until 1868 when Wylam Colliery, and hence also the waggonway, closed. However, in 1885 a large part of the line got a new lease of life when it was incorporated into North Eastern Railways' Scotswood, Newburn and Wylam branch line. This lasted until 1966, long enough to see diesel multiple units running, but was in effect a duplication of the Carlisle to Hexham route through Prudhoe along the southern bank of the Tyne.

The tracks were lifted in April 1972, which allowed construction of a bridleway along 4½ miles of the trackbed (GRs 163655 – 110642) from Newburn to Wylam Bridge. The best feature of the line, the delicately constructed bowstring Wylam Bridge, is perhaps best viewed from a passing train half a mile to the west of Wylam station, whilst the line also passes the cottage that was the birthplace of George Stephenson in 1781. Unfortunately, although owned by the National Trust, the cottage is not open to the public.

Holy Island Waggonway

Most people visiting Holy Island do so to see the priory or monastery founded by St Aidan in the seventh century, one of the great seats of Christian learning and home to the beautiful Lindisfarne Gospels. Adjacent to the ruins of the Benedictine monastery, destroyed by Henry VIII, is a visitor centre commemorating the life of the monks. The stones from the ministry were used to build the unforgettable Lindisfarne Castle. Less well known is the harbour area, where military fortifications (and a brewery) have been uncovered by archaeologists, and even less well known is Holy Island's tiny horse-drawn waggonway.

A number of lime kilns were built on the island in the 1860s by a Dundee firm. Lime had been burnt on the island since the end of the eighteenth century but on a much smaller scale. By the start of the twentieth century all workings on the island had ceased. Limestone was carried to the kilns by a horse-drawn (there is a suggestion that ponies rather than horses were used) waggonway from a quarry at the north end of the island. It was burnt with coal brought in by sea. One measure of coal was used to burn five measures of limestone. At one time five ships were carrying coal from Dundee to the island – clearly some sort of contractual arrangement as the Tyneside and Wearside pits were much nearer. The wooden pits of the jetty can be seen beyond the castle. An attractive feature of the waggonway is that is largely built on low embankments, presumably as

Junction of tramways on Holy Island. (Richard Lewis)

some form of protection against the encroachment of high tides, and therefore stands out clearly from the adjacent grassland. As a result, much of the waggonway's formation, including the site of a junction of two trackbeds and a bridge that the track crossed near the lime kilns may still be seen. After being burnt in the kilns the lime was then taken to the jetty on another waggonway, though the only rails visible today are those of the harbour slipway.

A number of other horse-drawn railways remain worth exploring in the North East, though many of the original routes were short, of wooden construction and left no remains, or else have been long since buried under the spread of urbanisation. Particularly worth further investigation are the Coxlodge (or Gosforth & Kenton) Waggonway to the north of the Tyne and the Team Valley to Pelaw route to the south of the same river.

Bibliography

The following books are recommended for further reading. It should be noted that whilst a number of them are either still in print or easily obtainable on the second-hand book market, others were printed in very small quantities, sometimes privately, and may now be very difficult to source.

Acton, R., *Exploring Cornwall's Tramway Trails* (volumes 1 and 2) (Troutbeck Press)

Anthony, G.H., *The Tavistock, Launceston & Princetown Railways* (Oakwood Press)

Baxter, B., *Stone Blocks and Iron Rails (Tramroads)* (David & Charles)

Bayliss, D.A., *Retracing the First Public Railway* (Living History Publications)

Bick, D.E., *The Gloucester & Cheltenham Railway* (Oakwood Press)

Boyd, J.I.C., *Narrow Gauge Railways in Mid Wales* (Oakwood Press)

Boyes, G., *The Heck Bridge and Wentbridge Railway* (Oakwood Press)

Burton, A., *Walking the Line* (Blandford Press)

Bushell, J., *The World's Oldest Railway* (Crown Press)

Cook, R.A. & Clinker, C.R. *Early Railways between Abergavenny and Hereford* (RCHS Publications)

Fairclough, A., *The Story of Cornwall's Railways* (Tor Mark Press)

Fernyhough, F., *The Liverpool & Manchester Railway 1830–1980* (Robert Hale)

Fletcher, M. & Taylor, J., *Railways – The Pioneer Years* (Studio Editions)

Guy, A. & Rees, J., *Early Railways 1569–1830* (Shire Publications)

Hemery, E., *Walking the Dartmoor Railroads* (David & Charles)

Inglis, J.C. & Inglis, F., *The Fordell Railway* (Privately published)

Kendall, H.G., *The Plymouth & Dartmoor Railway* (Oakwood Press)

Kidner, R.W., *The Railways of Purbeck* (Oakwood Press)

Lawson, P., *Walking the Dramway* (Tempus Publishing)

Lead, P., *The Caldon Canal & Tramroads* (Oakwood Press)

Marshall, J., *The Cromford & High Peak Railway* (David & Charles)

Martin, R., *North West Railway Walks* (Sigma Leisure Publishing)

Messenger, M. *Industrial Railways of the South West* (Twelveheads Press)

Metherall, J., *Pioneers & Preservation; Recording 200 Years of the Severn & Wye Railway* (Published by Dean Forest Railway Company)

Mortimer, I., *The Time Traveller's Guide to Medieval England* (Vintage Books)

Rattenbury, G., *Tramroads of the Brecknock & Abergavenny Canal* (RCHS Publications)

Rattenbury, G. & Cook, R., *The Hay & Kington Railways* (RCHS Publications)

Richards, S., *Railways from Llanelly* (Privately Published)

Ripley, D., *The Little Eaton Gangway* (Oakwood Press)

Ripley, D., *The Peak Forest Tramway* (Oakwood Press)

Russell, R., *Lost Canals & Waterways of Britain* (Sphere Books)

Statham, A. & Statham, C., *Talyllyn Railway Walks* (Published by Talyllyn Railway Company)

Stead, C., *The Birth of the Steam Locomotive – A New History* (Fern House)

Strathkelvin District Libraries & Museums, *The Monkland & Kirkintilloch Railway* (Privately Published)

Tolson, J.M., *The St Helens Railway* (Oakwood Press)

Townley, C.H.A., Smith, F.D. & Peden, J.A., *The Industrial Railways of the Wigan Coalfield* (Runpast Publishing)

Various authors, *Lost Railways* series (Countryside Books)

Vinter, J., *Vinter's Railway Gazetteer: A Guide to Britain's Old Railways that You Can Walk or Cycle* (The History Press)

Vinter, J., *Railway Walks* series (Wales, GWR &SR, LNER, LMR) (The History Press)

Webb, B. & Gordon, D.A., *Lord Carlisle's Railways* (RCTS Publications)